Career Leap Year

Melrose Public Library
Author Meet & Greet
2017

Career Leap Year

52 Ways To Reach
A New Level of Success

TOM CATALINI

Almianna Press

Career Leap Year: 52 Ways To Reach A New Level of Success

© 2016 by Tom Catalini
All Rights Reserved

ASIN: B01BB4YN4C

Cover Design by Boris Decovski

Published in the United States by Almianna Press

For My Family

SPECIAL BONUS!

Use the web address below to get a free PDF with all 52 Take Action! steps summarized neatly into one document for easy review...and action!

http://www.tomcatalini.com/CLYBonus

TABLE OF CONTENTS

INTRODUCTION

What if you could easily upgrade the skills that would help you to stand out in the crowd—at your workplace, in your industry, or among a field of job candidates?

What if you could more fully develop your leadership skills and your ability to wield influence? What if you could become a great public speaker? A great writer? A well-connected networker?

Would that open up more career opportunities for you?

You might find out.

You can improve your skills in all of these areas, because the only thing that matters is your level of commitment. Your potential is unlimited.

I will explain how this works.

Big skills are built little by little over time. An astronaut doesn't start out in space. A rock star doesn't start out on a major international tour. A CEO's first job isn't being CEO.

It's not about overnight success or one giant leap forward. It's about incremental improvements, consistently pursued over time.

That's how skills are built. Big skills. Skills that can give you a real advantage for growing your career.

You can make tremendous advances as long as you are willing to go toward them deliberately and persistently.

Which makes all of this completely within your reach.

In fact, right now, you are already way ahead of most people. You have already taken an important and necessary step in the right direction: you chose this book. You are reading right now about how to improve your skills.

As you work your way through the material in this book, as you try the suggestions for yourself, you will begin to see real results.

You will be glad you did. You will speak with greater confidence, write more compelling messages, and have a much larger professional network. All because you started today.

The specific insights in this book will help you reframe your thinking about work, improve your leadership capabilities, and build habits that will help you continue to grow for years to come.

The formula is simple:

Proven Insights + Your Deliberate Action = Your Personal Growth to New Heights.

I will provide the insight. I will fuel your inspiration. I will guide you on this journey. I will show you how the right mindset, approach, and action can take your professional development to the next level.

Why am I the best person to help you right now?

Because I've worked in all types of work environments, from the smallest startups to super-large Fortune 500 companies, from privately held to publicly traded, from my own entrepreneurial endeavors to prestigious nonprofits, from the private sector to the largest government agencies.

Across all of these environments, I have been testing ideas for career growth and advancement.

I've spent countless hours figuring out what works and what doesn't. Of course, I didn't just try things at random. I've researched this topic relentlessly, using the best social science available to inform my strategies and to understand *why* certain approaches work and others are doomed to fail.

Over the years, I have synthesized these learnings into writings, collected and published over years. Now the best of these writings are available to you in this curated collection.

Here's what to expect.

The first thing we'll look at is mindset. This book opens with a series of ideas on how you can think about your work and your professional development in bigger terms.

You are not here to paint within the lines or simply do what you are told. You are preparing to do more, deliver more, and craft a larger role for yourself. It's time to start thinking that way.

We will then explore many ideas on how to represent yourself well. The way you tell your own story, interact with others, and frame your discussions will help you establish a positive professional image. I'll get into the importance of finding your "tribe" as well as mentors to help you continue to grow over time.

Our work won't stop there. I will walk you through ideas on personal productivity, journaling, and using social media help you grow as well as develop and share your great ideas with the world.

Building on this, we will look at a variety of ideas on how to network, ways that you can improve how you connect with others and increase your influence. This is a look at communications at a personal level and how to handle interpersonal relationships in your work life.

We will then work on ways to improve your presentation and public speaking skills.

The ability to make a great presentation is crucial to your professional growth and career success. It will give you more confidence, make your more persuasive, and improve your credibility, whether you're in a job interview or making a presentation to coworkers or the board of directors.

Developing these skills doesn't have to be a scary or oversized challenge. It takes work and some discipline on your part, but it's not rocket science and it doesn't need to be an intimidating process. I'll give you lots of bite-sized (and big, if you want them) ideas to guide you along the way.

We'll look at writing too. We all have to do more of it than ever as part of our work now, but rarely stop to reflect on how we can do it more effectively. It's well worth considering. The payouts are huge in the long run.

Finally, we'll explore ideas on leadership. Professional growth means taking on leadership roles and increasing amounts of responsibility in this area, whether formally assigned or not.

Leadership is not about titles. It's about your ability to move things forward, for yourself and for the team. We'll look at the communication and leadership from a variety of angles, including often overlooked subtleties like body language.

As you can see, we are going to cover a lot of ground together. But don't worry — this is not a long and tedious book. It is designed to give you each of these 52 ideas in a simple, easily digestible, and highly actionable form. I've taken great care to present each individual idea as concisely as possible.

This way, you can read through all the ideas quickly and go back and forth through them at your leisure, focusing on whatever is most important to you at the moment.

I suggest picking one idea per week. If you work on just one idea per week diligently, over the course of a year, you will make tremendous progress in your professional development.

You are about to make a great investment in yourself. You are about to improve your current situation and prepare for new opportunities.

All of these habits and skills are 100% portable. As your career advances and evolves, the investments you make in your professional growth travel with you.

The potential is already inside you. You just need to unlock your own potential and put forth a consistent effort.

Let's go!

SECTION ONE
Mindset

1. COMPETENCE IS ONLY A STARTING POINT

W e spend a lot of time becoming (and staying) competent as professionals. No matter your area of specialty, you've put in the hours, days, weeks, months, and years to get good at what you do.

Here's the thing, though: competence alone is not enough if you want to get ahead.

Your reputation and influence are built on more.

People assume that you're competent at the specialized aspects of your work, or at least they'll usually give you the benefit of the doubt until you prove otherwise. They really can't easily measure your core competency directly. Which is why your connectedness matters.

Your ability to connect with others is crucial.

From small talk in the coffee line to long discussions at the company picnic, your personal interactions matter. Your style, mannerisms, sense of humor, habits, and hobbies all come into play to help others form an impression of you. You need to show some personality and also some personal traits that are important at work—dependability, trustworthiness, shrewdness, strong work ethic, and the like.

The other side of connectedness, of course, is getting to know others.

Paying attention to their styles and preferences, learning about their personal interests and families, and finding some common interests all help to form bonds. And the more you know each other, the more you'll be able to help each other achieve success, now and in the future.

This is your network.

Roles change, people leave the company, and new people join. But your connections remain, and your network of connections will prove invaluable to your career and your ability to get work done.

There are many tools and platforms to help you build, maintain, and leverage your connectedness these days. Social media platforms are great, and I'm a big fan of them. But real connectedness starts in person and right where you live and work every day.

The same is true for your staff, of course. So be sure to encourage them to be active in the work community. You need to ensure that others know about both their good work and their good nature. This will help you get them assigned to cross-functional teams, build greater trust and credibility for your group, and secure raises and promotions for your star performers as others get to know them the way you know them.

Competency is table stakes. Get connected to become a real player.

TAKE ACTION

Have as many non-work-related discussions as possible this week. Get to know your colleagues better as people, and let them get to know you better as a person.

2. LOGIC HAS ITS LIMITATIONS

Pure logic misses the mark when it comes to communications.

Most of the time, it's more important to be able to read between the lines. We need to understand what's not being said explicitly, what's not being well-articulated, what's motivating someone to try and shape an outcome.

The world is not a logical place and it's not filled with rational people. This is a major flaw in popular economic theory, and it can be a hurdle in how people approach problem solving.

We like to analyze a problem, understand the variables, and organize an orderly response. This approach has a lot of value. It helps us understand a situation, develop insights into core issues, and formulate a good plan. The danger is that any neat and tidy model of the world is an illusion.

Reality is much messier and far less certain.

People's behavior is difficult to predict, more variables are in play than what we can easily see, and we can't take everything that's said literally.

Not everyone says what they mean or means what they say — even if they try. Communication is usually more complicated. That's why it's worth investing time and energy to establish a rapport. To build a common understanding. To establish terminology. To ensure that everyone is "on the same page."

In work and in life, the things we discuss can mean different things to different people, and those meanings can even change over time. Paying careful, regular, and ongoing attention to this truth is important and worthwhile.

TAKE ACTION

Try speaking to someone on an emotional level about an issue rather than a logical level. Ask them how they feel about something rather than what they think about it.

3. DEVELOP YOUR STREET SMARTS

Gather better information and feedback (intelligence) from your audience in advance and you'll be well on your way to strengthening your ability to communicate effectively.

To be an effective communicator, you've got to have a good intake system. After all, what better way to shape the framing, tone, and content of what you say than to have it be well-informed by the raw data and color commentary of various constituents.

Knowing what you're up against is key. Some issues are controversial or divisive. Some are well-understood. Some don't even register in the zeitgeist. The more you understand these nuances, the better chance you have to construct and convey a message that is meaningful and influential.

What's more, we all suffer from the "curse of knowledge" — a cognitive bias where those who are closer to material on a particular topic find it very difficult to think about it from the perspective of those who are less well-versed in it. Going out and speaking and listening to others helps offset this shortcoming immensely.

Famed Harvard University Psychology Professor Steven Pinker describes the challenge and the solution quite well in a *Wall Street Journal* article, "The Source of Bad Writing":

"Social psychologists have found that we are overconfident, sometimes to the point of delusion, about our ability to infer what other people think, even the people who are closest to us. Only when we ask those people do we discover that what's obvious to us isn't obvious to them."

Of course, this challenge is found in all forms of communication, not just writing. Your speeches and presentations and even informal discussions with anyone outside the immediate circle of subject matter experts on a topic will benefit when you apply more attention and energy to getting a sense of what people do and do not know about your area of expertise.

Help yourself and help everyone else at the same time by working to overcome the curse of knowledge and learning more about how people think and feel about things as individuals before the group meets.

TAKE ACTION

Before your next meeting, go and talk to some of the individuals attendees in advance. Find out their thoughts and opinions before about the topic and see how that helps you when meeting time comes.

4. WORKING UNDER THE INFLUENCE

We all work under the influence of the masters who have come before us, or the ones who are alive and kicking right now.

We aim to emulate the best of what we see in pursuit of our own endeavors.

The key thing is to take those lessons and use them — but also create our own thing too.

We can study the way Steve Jobs gave a persuasive speech, but we shouldn't emulate him directly. We should let his example flow through our own individuality and come out in a new way (slightly modified or perhaps dramatically modified).

We should follow our inspirations and see where they lead. Often it's not really everything someone does or teaches us, but some specific thing that we find interesting.

We pick up something here, another thing there. We follow different threads and go down different paths.

Each of them may seem to go in varying and unrelated directions. That's OK.

They will all (or some, or most) come together in our interpretation, in our creation.

I'm inspired by Keith Richards (musically and otherwise), and this idea is very much some of my processing of the Netflix documentary *Keith Richards: Under the Influence* (a great title!).

It was fascinating to see all his musical influences and how they flow through him to create new things that are unique, and uniquely Keith.

We should all do the same in our own endeavors.

How can we put that to practice right now?

Start with awareness.

As you work through the next report you write, presentation you give, or meeting you hold, contemplate your influences.

Who in your personal life and readings and life lessons influence how you approach that work?

Think on it a bit and you might be surprised at what turns up in your mind. (If I think about my writing, I can see that some of my favorite bloggers and authors shine right through.)

Then, go a bit further and try to figure out what your secret sauce is. Where do your influences disappear and where does something uniquely you shine through? (I can see more of this in my own work now too, which is encouraging and helpful.)

Did you ever notice that you invented something new in the way you do a certain thing or that you form a particular combination of things in a way that nobody else does?

This is no doubt happening, but you probably are either giving yourself too much credit or not enough in some areas. It's helpful to try and break things down and see where the influences are and where you're creating new stuff.

Once you take notice, you can build on each effort more deliberately.

Be inspired, be unique.

TAKE ACTION

Identify your heroes. Who do you most want to emulate and why? Identify your unique capabilities. What can you do like nobody else?

SECTION TWO
Personal Development

5. WHAT'S YOUR STORY?

Tell it well and it will sell.

You've got a story to tell, and that's what people want to hear.

That's all they want to hear, really.

In fact, people are so primed to hear your story that if you don't tell them one, they'll fill in the blanks themselves and decide what your story is.

It's better that you control the narrative yourself.

Craft a clear, concise, and compelling story and you'll go a long way toward convincing and cajoling whoever is listening to your pitch to help you create the outcomes you most desire.

Let's look at an extreme example: interviewing for a new job.

Landing a job or hiring an employee are dramatic moments for the candidate and manager alike. What does each want to know most?

They want to know each other's story.

As a candidate, you want to know what the story is with this place, the position, and the people. What's the narrative and do you fit into it? That's how you'll decide if this is the right "fit" for you.

As a hiring manager, you want to know the candidate's story. Where do they come from? Who do they aspire to become? How have they managed their professional journey so far, and will they fit well with the team, the organization, and the plans you have in the works?

Each wants to know the other's story and how they might fit together.

That's the bottom line.

That's the essential question underlying all the kerfuffle of the hiring process.

What's your career story?

Sooner or later you will be contemplating your next career move. But even if you aren't, crafting the narrative of your career can help you better understand some of your specific personal aspirations.

Understanding your own story in this way can help you re-approach your current work and gain greater satisfaction and success even if you're not changing jobs.

Dust off your resume. Spend a week on it. Take a look at the major milestones and consider the arc of your career.

As you look at each job change, promotion, or significant project, the key question to ask is: as you worked on each challenge, how did you change as a result?

For instance, when a colleague and I started a technology consulting business many years ago, it was because we loved technology and we were good at working with it. We mastered all the hot technologies of the day and could leverage that knowledge to make money.

In order to do the work, though, I had to learn how to sell. The business owners who bought the work didn't care about technology, they cared about business results. They paid money for value, not for technology.

I had to totally change the way that I communicated. I learned a lot, mostly through lots of trial and error.

The way that experience changed me prepared me for future steps in my career as a strategist and executive when communicating and thinking along those lines were of paramount importance.

Each of my career transitions has some sort of change like that. Each of your transitions does too. That's a good place to start to build your career narrative.

What challenges have you faced? How did you change as a result? How did that prepare you to meet new challenges?

Figure out your story. Then you will be able to tell it well. And it will sell. (Even if you're only selling to yourself.)

TAKE ACTION

Craft your career story. At each step or major milestone, answer the question, "How did you change as a result?" Be able to tell it in two minutes or less.

6. HAVE YOU FOUND YOUR TRIBE?

Early in my career as an IT consultant I found the value of learning from peers. Communities would form, largely around enterprise technology vendors.

These user groups were a way for those of us in IT to connect with each other and learn from each other.

We'd share stories of configuration challenges, implementation strategies, and tons of tips and tricks for coercing the technology into working effectively.

Participating in these groups gave me a tremendous advantage in my career. I'd gain practical knowledge and insights not readily available anywhere else, and I'd apply it to my work regularly.

These groups also gave me incentive to develop my own work further, because I always wanted to give back to the community by sharing knowledge and insights of my own.

Then I got lost...

As I grew into leadership and management roles, there was less value for me in these technical groups and there was less that I could offer. I struggled along for a while, feeling my way through the new challenges of management.

I had to go it alone, as did many of us who grew into these roles without the benefit of formal training, mentorship, or guidance.

...until I found new peer groups.

Connecting with others who faced the same struggles was again an enormous boon to my career.

The central discussions shifted from technical matters to management matters, but the value of the exchange was the same as before: I gained knowledge and insights not found anywhere else.

The information came once again from a lively and interactive dialogues with experienced professionals facing similar challenges.

These dialogues became a thread for forming relationships over time. And many of these relationships evolved into trusted, reliable sources of inspiration, advice, mentorship, and friendship.

I've continued to derive enormous value from interacting with peers, which has been a great benefit to my career. Applying these lessons helps me do better work. And I continue to be inspired to raise my game, try new things, and develop lessons that I can share with my peer communities.

We're very fortunate that today, more than ever before, the act of finding and participating in our tribes is much easier. They can take the form of email lists, groups on social media platforms, blogs, videocasts, podcasts, and more. And good old-fashioned face-to-face networking groups are alive and thriving.

My best career advice for leaders always includes a recommendation to find and actively participate in professional groups.

Being a go-getter who hangs out with other go-getters will make you more likely to find success and will help others find it too.

TAKE ACTION

Find at least three groups that might be helpful to developing your career and personal growth. Actively participate in all three groups. Pick at least one group and attend every meeting for the next few months.

7. REPUTATION MANAGEMENT

"When it comes to defining yourself and your ideas, the key is not to abdicate responsibility to others who don't deserve the privilege."

— Kathleen Kelley Reardon

In other words, if you don't manage your reputation, others will. And you may not like how it takes shape.

We're busy with lots of work. The stakes are high and lots of attention to detail is required. But the work is not just about the work. Much of what we do is all about working with people. It's in those interactions that our reputations are defined.

What you say, how you say it, your body language, demeanor, and tone of voice all shape how others perceive you. We can't spend all our energy managing all of these details all the time, of course. Many moments, though, merit some attention to how your reputation is formed.

Interactions with your boss or subordinates, a meeting with a vendor, discussions with stakeholders from other departments, the times you lead a meeting or make a presentation — these are all opportunities to shape how others see you, to help them see and understand you clearly and in the manner you would like. To emphasize certain aspects of your personality, approach, and unique value proposition. To build your personal brand.

In all of these situations, we have more control over perceptions than we might think. Take control in how you initiate — and respond — to circumstances, to shape your identity and personal brand the way you would like them to be shaped.

TAKE ACTION

Identify three words that best describe the image you want to portray. Think about ways you can embody those words. Think about specific actions you can take to begin to help others see you in this light. Take those actions.

8. DO YOU HAVE AT LEAST ONE GOOD MENTOR?

It doesn't matter how experienced and knowledgeable you are. It doesn't matter what your title is. It doesn't matter what certifications you've earned or which awards you've won....

We all need guidance.

It can come from someone more experienced in your field, your industry, or your area of specialization. But it can also come from many other places.

Good guidance has only three requirements: It should be focused on your best interest. It should be focused on helping you achieve results. It should be focused on helping you both do the right thing and do the thing right.

Finding and asking for help can seem daunting, but often it's surprisingly easy to pull off.

Sometimes all you need to do is ask.

There are two truths working in your favor: people are flattered when you ask them for advice, and people like to talk about what they know.

This makes an opening quite easy. A good inquiry might go something like this: "I'd love to get some career advice from you. Would you be willing to share how you got to where you are today?"

If you open up a dialogue like that with some people that you admire, respect, and would like to learn from, you will be well on your way to finding some good mentors.

Of course, you need to keep in mind the three rules above. You are looking for someone who will actively participate in your success by providing good guidance on specific matters over time.

I've been fortunate to land some truly awesome mentors over the years. They've helped me through difficult challenges and also shared in the celebration of my successes.

As a result of their generosity, I am inspired to pay it forward and hope I have been similarly valuable to those who I have mentored.

If you are in a leadership role, you likely don't have many (or any) peers who face the same challenges as you do in your organization.

This fact won't preclude you from finding a good mentor within your organization, but it does mean that there is also tremendous value in finding a mentor outside of your organization too.

It's also always good to have more than one mentor. The variety of perspectives and insights and experience you will gain through multiple mentors is tremendously valuable.

Go out and find some help. And don't forget to help others too. You will make a good mentor.

TAKE ACTION

Make a list of ten potential mentors from your personal network. These should be people that you admire and that you can learn from. Reach out to three of them this week and ask if you can treat them to coffee or lunch and discuss career strategies.

9. PUTTING YOURSELF OUT THERE

The ways we handle ourselves in difficult scenarios and take advantage of opportunities shape our professional image. People see us in a certain way based on how we represent ourselves in all these different circumstances.

So does the rest of the world.

You can remain hidden, of course. By not participating on common social networks like LinkedIn, Twitter, and Facebook, you will remain largely out of view.

In that case, the rest of the world does not see you at all. Unless you've perhaps gained some notoriety in the press or other media outlets. But your influence over that sort of thing is, of course, limited.

Putting yourself out there, in a way that's fully under your control, is often a better way to manage your online presence. After all, don't you want the rest of the world to see you? And to see your best self?

Consider how your presence (or lack of it) plays out when you're looking for a new job. Who would you expect to have a better shot at a leadership position—someone who is invisible online or someone who is curating and authoring thought leadership in their industry?

The same issues are true if you are looking to attract the best talent. Who would you expect the best in your industry to want to work for—someone who is totally inaccessible except by way of an arranged meeting by gatekeepers or someone who is actively and openly engaged in the discourse of their profession?

Less obvious than those examples, perhaps, is the case for a particularly relevant aspect of professional development for today's leaders....

Participating in the various forums of engagement that the Internet provides is a great way to learn about the forums themselves. To see how the various platforms work. To experience the different user interfaces. To understand the mechanics and the configurations. To learn the decorum of each community. To figure out where the good stuff is at and how the smartest people experiment and leverage the platforms for a variety of purposes.

For leaders in the digital era, I would argue that this is an essential skill. What better way to position yourself to be a meaningful contributor to these conversations in your organization than by becoming literate through firsthand experience?

And what better place to be seen doing that than right out in the open where you're likely to cross paths with others who are exploring the leading edge themselves?

TAKE ACTION

Write a post and publish it on your favorite social network. Share an idea, an insight, a hope, a dream about something that is important to you.

10. PRODUCTIVITY BINGE

Do you ever go on a productivity binge?

I'm not productive all the time, but I do go on productivity binges from time to time. Sometimes I can't even tell when I've entered that zone until I get a clue from someone else.

That someone else was once the guy at a local cafe, a place that I had been going to for about a week.

I knew something was up when the guy at my "new" place knew my complete order and my name as soon as I walked in. I had gone from anonymity to regular in less than a week.

"Hi, Tom. Would you like a falafel rollup with hummus today, for here?"

Uh, yes I would, but how did you know that?

Well, in my short time visiting the new establishment, I had shown up at the same time and ordered the same thing every day.

I was particularly busy that week, working in a focused manner toward a set of very specific goals. When that happens, I tend to shut down lots of small decisions for things that aren't so important.

Things like where and when to go to lunch and what to eat and many other routines throughout the day become ritualistic. Minimizing focus on these less important things allows me to focus more attention, energy, and decision making on the tasks that I've made a priority.

I don't do this all the time. In fact, I make a point of breaking routines when creative thinking is a priority. But when massive productivity is needed, routine is king.

TAKE ACTION

Determine something simple that you can create a routine around this week. Follow that routine diligently for the entire week. See how it feels to free yourself from those little decisions on a regular basis.

11. DONE IS BETTER THAN PERFECT

A ll projects are not created equal.

But it can be hard not to treat them that way.

My many projects span personal and professional realms. Some are big, others small. Some are simple, some are complex. Cheap/expensive, time-consuming/quick...you get the idea.

They all have one thing in common, however. They all require decisions.

I try not to hem and haw on those decisions, but it seems my default nature is to consider all the decisions equally.

I'm an analyst and debater.

It's fun and interesting to look at things from various angles, to consider the possibilities, to find creative and comprehensive solutions.

Striving for perfection is challenging, but it's not productive.

So, I fight the perfectionism urge by taking action.

My backyard fence is a good example.

It is fine structurally, but the paint keeps peeling. This creates a lot of maintenance work because the fence has a nice design with lattice at the top.

It became clear that replacing the fence panels with unpainted wood would be a better path forward. I could spend time replacing the panels instead of scraping paint and then I'd be maintenance free going forward.

The challenge is that this opened up a lot of options.

What type of wood should I use? Should I use wider or narrower boards? Should I use lattice again or change the design? What other design options should I consider? What are the pros and cons? Etc., etc., etc.

I got advice from my brother, who is an expert carpenter, and my neighbor, who is an artist and also a craftsman himself. Google and the interwebs helped too.

This led to many great insights and ideas, and also to more questions and more decisions to consider.

A path to analysis paralysis....

The thing I realized is among the project I'm working on, this one doesn't require perfection. I don't need to solve my fence problem for all possible current and future scenarios. I just need to get the project done.

So I took action. Because done is better than perfect.

Once decisive action is taken, things start to happen. It forces more decisions to happen. Things quickly begin to take shape.

Once I took down a section of the fence, I had to figure something out.

Once I was at Home Depot I bought supplies from the choices available.

Once I started to build the fence section back up, I had to make decisions about the final design.

Once the design was set for one section of the fence, it just needs to be replicated.

Imperfection reigns over this project. It turns out, for instance, that the boards aren't all exactly straight, the fence structure hasn't aged gracefully in some areas, and I simply don't know the proper techniques to build the fence like a craftsman (Dammit Jim, I'm a writer not a builder!).

I see this imperfection now. I can even see it when I look out the window from 30 feet away...I'm spotting small spacing or alignment issues...and they do bother me...I do wish the fence was perfect right now.

That's because I'm currently deep in the project.

When it's done, it'll be fine and I won't obsess about these small issues. I'll just have a nice fence that I don't need to spend time worrying about or maintaining.

And I'll be on to the next project. Which will feel great.

TAKE ACTION

Get one thing done this week that you've been hemming and hawing about. Let go of perfection and get it over the finish line!

12. TIME AND ATTENTION

W e all try to manage time carefully. There are exactly 24 hours in a day and they're going to pass by no matter how we use them.

I'm not the most efficient or productive person, but I do try to be intentional with my time.

The thing I'm learning, though, is that it's equally (if not more) important to consider how I manage my attention.

After all, I can use my time to attend a meeting, but my attention can be elsewhere. I can be thinking of where to go to lunch, how I'm going to prepare for another meeting, or I can be reading and writing email.

This is a challenge even when working alone in a rare quiet moment because there is a need to fight the Pavlovian response to notifications of all kinds.

Everything wants to notify me, it seems. The apps don't just want my time, they are demanding my attention.

Some of the stuff I'm notified about is important. Some is interesting. Some is fun or funny.

Just like one of Pavlov's dogs, I'm conditioned to respond. The buzzer is heavily associated with some kind of treat.

Fighting this urge, however, is becoming an increasingly crucial strategy in managing my attention.

Taking stock of the "signal to noise ratio" or how many of the notifications are actually important makes it clear that most of the stuff literally doesn't suffer one bit if my attention to it is delayed for a few minutes...or even a few hours.

Still, it can be difficult to resist the urge to see what the notification is about.

So, I put the phone aside when I want to manage my attention more carefully. If I go to a meeting without it, there is no urge to respond to a notification because there is no notification. Moreover, I can't check my phone for any reason because it isn't there.

It works like a charm. Whether for a meeting, a lunch gathering, or working alone on a project, if I don't have my phone I can better sync up how I'm spending my attention more with how I'm spending my time.

When there is something on your calendar that is important to you — a big meeting, an important lunch, or your kid's soccer game — and you want to be more fully present, go there with your time and your attention. Leave the phone in your coat, in your office, or in your car.

See what you notice when you're fully present rather than worry about notifications that will only distract you from fully being there.

TAKE ACTION

Go to at least one meeting or perform one important task or spend at least one hour each day this week without your phone.

13. WHY YOU SHOULD TAKE NOTES FROM YOURSELF

Listen to yourself. You're pretty smart.

We take notes in all sorts of circumstances — at meetings, at conferences, while reading books, during class, and more.

We want to capture the gems that others are sharing with us so that we can put them to good use later.

We can reflect on the key points, internalize them, and take action when the time is appropriate.

We do all this because it is worth capturing ideas, insights, tips, and tricks.

So why not take notes from yourself?

You are full of ideas and insights, tips and tricks. Why not capture those things so that you can share them with others?

Perhaps more importantly, though, you can capture them for yourself.

Jotting down well-formed or nascent ideas or thoughts can help you stow away things for later use or reflect on and develop them further.

The beauty is that you get to look back and see your thoughts again. This helps with memory, of course, but also with developing things further.

You can start to connect dots, perhaps applying an idea from one area of your life to another.

You can boost your confidence by acknowledging that you have more ideas than you think you do, accomplish more than you think, or have more well-formed future plans than you think.

Odds are you are doing better than you give yourself credit for; reflecting on your notes can help you to see things more clearly.

You can better see ideas that you should share with others. You see more ways that you can be helpful.

You can get better at remembering things. You can more easily prioritize things. You can have better information to think more strategically.

Try it out.

Find a moment of pause or two each day to capture some thoughts in a notes app or on a sheet of paper. Just put down whatever is rolling around in your mind.

Don't worry about format or congruency...just dump stuff out.

Put the next big business idea down right next to the reminder to pick up the dry cleaning and your idea for the next movie you want to watch and the four bullet points on the opening slide of your next presentation and your idea for a great meeting topic.

Later you will go back and look at everything and worry about next steps or processing or re-organizing. The point now is to just capture your thoughts.

When it's time to look back and see what you've accumulated, you'll likely conclude that it was more than you thought possible. And this little review session has probably given you more helpful insights than you would have with a pre-edited output of ideas.

And yeah, you do have moments of pause throughout each day. While you're waiting for a meeting or conference call to start, while you're waiting in line for a sandwich, while you're riding the train or the elevator, and probably many other tiny little slots. Capitalize on those opportunities.

You'll figure it out. You're pretty smart. Which is why you're worth listening to and taking notes.

TAKE ACTION

Carry a pocket-sized notebook and pen or pencil with you everywhere you go for the entire week. Jot down notes and ideas and random thoughts whenever they come to mind. Review the full set of notes at the end of the week.

14. WHY LISTS SHOULD BE PART OF YOUR SELF IMPROVEMENT

Have you ever gone all the way to the grocery store and back, only to realize that you forgot a critical ingredient?

The cure, of course, is to use a list. Put things on the list before you go and check them off as you put them in your cart.

If a trip to the grocery store can be thrown off track by the lack of a list, imagine what happens at a busy workplace when you don't have a written plan of attack.

List are great in many ways....

1. Lists make things simple and clear. Before you can add an item to a list, you need to decide exactly what it is. The need for brevity forces you to clarify the definition of the item so that you can write it down.

2. Lists help you see the big picture. You need to break things down to their component parts in order to make the list. Once the list is built, you are able to more easily see everything end to end and how the pieces fit together.

3. Lists help you plan and prioritize. Now that you can see all the pieces, you can think things through before taking action. You can evaluate and assess different sequencing options, priorities, and strategies in order to determine the best path forward.

4. Lists make you more efficient. Once you're taking action, the list can keep you on track. Do one thing, then the next. The well-

41

developed list allows you to focus on execution.

5. Lists are motivating. They can provide a great sense of accomplishment as you work through them. You can see progress as you check things off. You can get a sense of how far you've come and how close you are to completion.

6. Lists provide mental freedom. You can stop worrying about trying to remember things — it's all written down. Focus your energy on the task at hand; the list will dutifully hold everything else until you're ready.

That's a pretty good list, don't you think?

TAKE ACTION

Make a list of action items every day this week. Create the list in the morning and check it at the end of every day.

SECTION THREE

Connecting with Others

15. THE ONE WHO LISTENS FIRST WINS

Can you hear me now?

That's what everyone is thinking. Particularly in intense, emotionally charged, or otherwise fragile communication situations.

Most of the time we obsess about what we're going to say next, how we are going to say it, and the ways we want to sway the other person to our point of view.

In some situations, however, the exact opposite approach is far more effective.

Listening is the winning strategy.

Before people will hear you, they want to be heard.

I know this is true, because I know that I want to be heard. And I know this is true because when I shut up and listen (and really pay attention), it usually leads to much better results.

I also know that when I listen, I hear opportunities. They are right there in front of me, out in the open, waiting to be leveraged (in a good way).

When you actively listen, you can more accurately hear what the other person is saying. And they will present openings.

They will reveal their true thoughts and concerns. They will reveal their hopes. They will tell you where the place is to leverage for a more meaningful connection.

These things won't necessarily be explicitly stated, of course. That's why you'll miss them if you're not looking for them.

Your job as a listener is to see and seize those opportunities. That's how you win. And, yes, the other person wins too. That's the point.

We don't want to win at their expense, we want to win by finding common links to whatever solutions you're both after. The solution (or more accurately, the problem) is often not that obvious at the outset. It only emerges when real dialogue is occurring.

You can try this out for yourself.

In an upcoming conversation or meeting, focus on what the other person is saying. Let go of any inner dialogue about how you're going to respond or what you're going to say next. Just listen.

Listen carefully and know that you will be able to respond or make your next point when the time comes. You don't need to prepare for it as much as you think you do.

Look at improv comedy. The whole point is that nothing is prepared in advance. People are responding in the moment and they can only respond after listening—there is no script. There is no need for a script.

Sure, sometimes it works better than others. That's OK. Most of the time it works extremely well. Things that never could have been anticipated or scripted emerge...that's the magic.

When you're not quite sure what's going to happen next or how you should respond, listening is the winning strategy.

TAKE ACTION

Approach conversations this week like an improv actor. Do not even think about what you are going to say until the other person has completely finished speaking. Listen completely to everything they say.

16. HAVING A DIALOGUE

Many of us like to be efficient and we like technology. So, email is a natural and effective way for us to communicate. Most of the time, we're either communicating in a meeting or by email (and sometimes we're doing both at the same time!).

But those two forums alone are not enough. One of the most powerful communications tools in our arsenal is the one-on-one conversation.

Unlike any other type of discussion, this one is a true dialogue. One person speaks, and then the other one responds. For better or worse, there's no place to hide.

There's no third (or fourth or fifth) party that needs catering to in any way. There's no forwarding of messages or "reply all" chain. There's just two people exchanging information, ideas, and insights—live and in real time. Tackling tough questions, sharing a laugh, developing plans.

These discussions tend to be very productive (in a variety of ways—getting real work done, building rapport, developing trust). And even when they're not particularly productive, I still usually find them to be revealing in some way. Which makes them worthwhile.

The one-on-one discussion can foster relationships with stakeholders and constituents across organizations. These conversations can also help strengthen our most crucial connections within the business units. It's always good to have a regular dialogue going with a bunch of different people at work.

Grab lunch. Meet for coffee. Drop by an office. Schedule a conference room.

It's important to do this, I've found, even when we're busy (and especially when we're busy).

TAKE ACTION

Transition one conversation each day this week from email to another format. Pick up the phone, drop by, or arrange an appointment.

17. TEACHING AND LEARNING

Nothing crystallizes understanding like the process of teaching.

After all, how often do we revisit things we already know? Usually, we take them for granted and we focus on learning new things instead.

But when we have the opportunity to help someone else learn new things, we are able to learn too. Teaching is a great way to learn.

When you need to help someone understand something, it forces you to structure your thoughts, ideas and experiences into a cohesive story. You've got to be able to articulate it well when you explain it to someone else. You need to be able to break it down into its component parts and help the other person see how and why they fit together.

You've got to slow down and be deliberate. You've got to engage the other person in a thoughtful and organized and patient manner.

To prepare for that discussion, you essentially force yourself to see something for the first time again. This allows you the opportunity to think holistically about it and to revisit its fundamental concepts. Re-examining the familiar from this perspective can really help to deepen your own understanding. It can help you to uncover new insights.

The person you are teaching will help you see it anew too. They will ask you basic questions, unexpected questions, and nuanced questions, forcing you to examine the topic from new angles. They will offer a unique perspective, new opinions, and new insights. All of this can help to solidify and shape your own understanding further.

Teaching is an act of generosity, but it's a self-serving act too. Both people benefit.

It's a great way to build rapport with someone. It's a great way to ensure a shared understanding of something. It's a great way to look at something again for the first time.

TAKE ACTION

Teach someone something this week. Explore the best way to present the topic, to organize the concepts, to convey understanding and insight. Then, teach it to them and see what you learn in the process.

18. HOW DO YOU HANDLE HALLWAY CONVERSATIONS?

You know those informal meetings where you bump into an individual or two and chat more openly and directly than you do when sitting around the conference table. Do you prepare for those encounters or just wing it?

I try to figure out how to best leverage the opportunity to learn and to share, should I get a chance to catch someone in a more intimate, less formal setting. Conversations in the hallway, the parking lot, or around the coffee machine are often more revealing than discussions in a conference room. The surroundings are less formal and more relaxed, and people tend to be more open when there are less people around.

Of course, you never know who you're going to bump into or when these encounters might happen, but you can give some thought to the key issues you might cover if the opportunity arises. Perhaps you want to better understand someone's motivations, concerns, or relationships to others. Knowing what they really think about a particular issue can be helpful to clearing logjams and keeping things moving forward.

Similarly, I find it helpful to think about the key points I'd want to convey directly to people. It's helpful to know what your specific talking points would be, how you'd like to help someone frame their thinking on a particular issue, or concerns you'd like to share but hesitate to raise in a larger group or a more formal setting.

Informal communications are where a lot of action takes place. While we focus a lot of energy on formal communications channels, I think it's also helpful to sometimes be intentional about informal channels.

TAKE ACTION

Strike up at least one informal conversation per day this week as you come across colleagues. Make a point of moving beyond polite small talk and discussing something more substantive.

19. SAY YES TO EVERYTHING

What if we just said yes immediately and enthusiastically?

I don't mean to say that we should just blindly accept new initiatives. We can't do that. That will lead to chaos and disappointment.

We can say yes to listening, however. We can accept all ideas for consideration. We can make sure that the person who comes to us excitedly is heard. We can agree to a discussion where we help to understand the problem they are trying to solve or the opportunity they are trying to leverage.

Saying yes is an opportunity. We'll learn more about the business at hand. We'll get a sense of why this issue has come up and what strategies are being considered for moving forward. This openness is a great way to get a finger on the pulse of what's important to the business in this moment, and to get an understanding of why it's important.

Taking time for this conversation is also a great way to deepen relationships with business partners. People appreciate being listened to and helped. And we'll be able to share our knowledge and insights by asking thoughtful questions and helping them think things through.

We may end up resizing or reshaping the idea, or even having to delay or say no to the initiative. That's OK. The answer is important, but it's even more important that the answer is well-reasoned and clearly understood.

Devote some time and attention to fully hearing the person out, collaborate and commiserate with them, and educate and advise them properly. It helps to be seen as a person to go to with ideas, a person who will listen, a person who offers insight and advice and help.

TAKE ACTION

Don't say no to any requests this week. Instead, hold open the possibility that you might be able to help. Use the opportunity to spend time listening more deeply about what is being asked.

20. THE ART OF DE-ESCALATION

When making an important presentation or giving a talk, we want to use emotion to command attention and spur action. In many everyday circumstances, however, we need to move in the other direction.

Sometimes emotions run high, for a variety of reasons. Many of the reasons are well outside of our control.

But we can control our response. And we can put things onto a more constructive path.

Whether it's an upset person trying to get help desk support, an outburst at a project meeting, or an inter-departmental scuffle gone awry, what we need to do next is clear. We need to remove the emotion from the situation.

Reducing things to a pattern of indisputable facts goes a long way. We'll have to dig for some of these facts and dodge some emotionally charged obstacles along the way. We'll have to de-personalize statements, ignore innuendos, and absorb a little frustration while people vent. But eventually we'll get to the bottom of things.

My consulting background serves me well in this regard. In that role in my formative years, I always had to be objective, professional, and clearly focused on business outcomes. That approach works well in these situations.

Even if you haven't been a consultant, you can simply think of yourself more as an observer than a participant. Set yourself apart from the situation a bit. Notice what is happening and move through it, but don't react and don't judge. Just observe.

You can analyze and form opinions later, after the dust settles and the emotional heat dissipates. Getting yourself caught up in the emotions of the moment doesn't help you or anyone else.

If you're the one seeing clearly, you will see the path forward. You will show others the way. And you will earn their respect and support.

Cool, calm, and collected is a good way to see. And a good way to be seen.

TAKE ACTION

As something heats up and emotions start to run high, remain objective. Take a deep breath and decide that you are going to avoid getting emotionally entangled in the moment. If that's just not possible, take a break and go for a short walk to blow off some steam in private.

21. WHERE ARE THEY COMING FROM?

It can be instinctive to jump to conclusions when someone is talking to us, and that's influenced a lot by where we think they're coming from. Are they coming from a good place, trying to help and offer support, suggestions, and insight? Or are they coming from a not-so-good place, trying to gather information and inject ideas to skew things in the direction of their personal agenda?

If we assume the latter, we may shut down our listening skills to our own detriment. When we shut down so quickly, we lose an opportunity to learn. What if the person is actually trying to help? What if they are saying something important and you're not hearing it?

If you assume positive intent, you will hear things differently. More completely. You'll engage more directly, ask follow up questions, consider the point more carefully.

Rather than spend a lot of cycles figuring out whether someone is coming from a good or bad place, sometimes it's best to just assume its all good, that they're doing the best they can, and listen very carefully. To take in and try to understand as much as possible.

How you listen doesn't mean that you're compelled to respond in a certain way. If you decide later that the person's intent was not positive, you can respond appropriately (and be armed with better information).

TAKE ACTION

Give the other person the benefit of the doubt this week. Assume that they are coming from a place of genuine concern and that they have only the best of intentions as you listen to them.

22. WHY DO QUESTIONS GET MORE ATTENTION?

If I asked you a question, what would you say?

You'd give me an answer of some sort, because questions are to be answered. That's our cultural norm.

And because I've posed a question and you're expected to answer, I've caused you to think about the topic we're discussing in a very different way than if I had just told you something.

Questions are engaging. They take us from monologue to dialogue. They create a deeper discussion than throwing statements around. And they cause us to think together more deliberately; they encourage us to collaborate.

If you answered my question, you'd likely ask me a question back, wouldn't you?

Of course, for us to get anywhere meaningful in this conversation, we'd have to ask each other good questions—ones that sparked critical thinking and analysis.

What if you approached even a project status meeting with a good line of questioning?

Instead of an agenda of topics or tasks to review, you could ask some deeper questions. Perhaps something like:

"What was one surprising thing you learned this week that could change how we think about some of the future aspects of the project?"

or

"Why did things go well with [task X] or [obtaining person Y's approval]?" (asking about why something went right instead of why something went wrong)

Or perhaps you could ask some team members to pose questions instead of stating updates.

TAKE ACTION

Eliminate bland status update questions from all of your meetings this week. Instead, ask creative questions that will yield more insightful answers.

23. THE INFORMATIONAL INTERVIEW

Take the meeting.

Whether someone offers you an opportunity for an informational interview or whether someone asks if you can hold one as a favor to a friend or colleague.

This is networking at its essence.

Professional development is most profound outside of the four walls of whatever organization you're in at the moment.

Get outside and meet people.

Welcome others into your world.

It may be called an "informational interview" or go by some other name; what I'm talking about is that one-on-one networking opportunity that we pursue all too infrequently. Mostly, we do it when we're looking for a new job or contemplating a career change. We should be doing this all the time, for lots of other reasons.

When the opportunity arises, take it.

If you are to be the primary beneficiary of the meeting, the mentee if you will, then you have before you a fantastic opportunity to learn from someone else.

You have a chance to listen to yourself summarize your situation and articulate your goals. You have a chance to learn about and benefit from someone else's experience and see the world from a new perspective. You have a chance to meet more people, to dramatically expand your network.

Go in prepared. Be vulnerable. Listen, learn, and explore a world of new ideas and possibilities by asking lots of questions.

If you will be the host of the meeting, to be a mentor of sorts, then do your best to help as much as possible.

Ask lots of questions, and then lots of follow-up questions. Be sure that you put a lot of time and energy into understanding the person's situation and their aspirations.

You are helping tremendously by putting them through the paces. Listening to themselves respond to your probing questions is probably going to be more helpful than any bit of wisdom you may impart directly. The meeting is not about you, it's about them.

Now, the important part.

Follow up. Don't let this new connection fade away. The point of the meeting is not the meeting itself, but the new connection.

Cultivate it and expand it. One meeting should lead to further discussions, additional meetings, and most certainly to additional connections through referrals for more informational interviews.

That is networking far more powerful than anything you'll ever find on LinkedIn or industry conference.

So, take action.

A good thing to do would be to schedule a get-together with a colleague. Get a date on the calendar for some one-on-one networking with someone you know. Talk to them about some area of personal professional development, some area you'd like to learn more about or improve on. Ask if they can arrange an informational interview with someone in their network.

This could kickstart a nice opportunity to expand your network and your horizons a bit.

And, by all means, if someone asks if a friend or colleague can meet you to learn about your career/organization/experience/ whatever, say yes.

TAKE ACTION

Accept any and all requests you get for an informational interview. If you are not receiving requests, make requests of your own. Reach out to at least three people this week and ask if you can interview them over coffee.

SECTION FOUR
Presentation Skills

24. HOW TO SHOW AND TELL AND PERSUADE

Tell us about the destinations but show us the journey.

When you have an idea to share with others and you want them on board with where you are going, think about it this way: It's nice to know that you found a great destination. And it's nice to know all about it. It's nice to have you show us around.

We want to know the details of what it looks like, what it feels like, what it sounds like, what it smells like, and what it tastes like. All five senses!

This will help us to know why the destination is so wonderful, what you will be able to do there, and how it will be included in future plans.

Those details may influence our own decision making. After all, we listen attentively to stories for very selfish reasons. Mostly because the information might be directly relevant to us in the future.

That's why stories are a crucial tool for persuasion.

But if you want your story to be truly persuasive, you must adhere to the old writing adage:

Show, don't tell.

That doesn't mean using ultra-descriptive language to invoke the five senses, even though some of that can be helpful. And it doesn't mean adding images and video and sound to invoke them either.

It means you must show us your reasoning.

Sure, we do want to know all about the destination, but more importantly, we want to know how you got there.

We want to know the motivation and reasoning for all the choices made along the way. We want to know the implications of those choices. We want to know how you reacted to those things. We want to know how your choices added new twists and turns, what you chose to do next, and why.

That's the real story. That's what we want you to show us.

Telling = conclusions.

Showing = how you arrived at conclusions.

The show, don't tell writing adage can serve as a crucial tool of persuasion. Whether you are writing, speaking, or delivering a presentation, we want to hear a story. And we want to know the emotional journey as much as (more than) all of the sensory details.

Learning about choices and implications and follow-up choices drives interest and engagement because they put us vicariously in the driver's seat. That's just where we want to be sitting when we hear a good story.

You may have already arrived at the destination, or you may be encouraging us to select a new destination. You may be offering a choice of multiple possible destinations.

We want to hear all about those.

But we won't be riding along with you very long if you don't share the essential elements of the story: why we are on the journey and why we are making particular choices.

TAKE ACTION

Practice telling stories of how you arrived at certain conclusions this week. It could be personal or work related. Include choices and reasons for those choices as well as emotions. Put your listener in the driver's seat.

25. AMAZING GRAPES AND USEFUL STORIES

You are surrounded by good stories — stories that you can put to good use.

Stories are one of the best ways to get your message across, to set up your talking points, to help people internalize what you are trying to explain. They can be an effective way to frame any discussion.

I used the business turnaround story of a California wine store called Amazing Grapes to set up my keynote talk for a conference on social media.

The story was all about adapting a business model to our evermore social world, creating higher value for customers and more revenue for the business.

In the case of Amazing Grapes, the social adjustment was made by renovating the store and using an entirely new layout, making way for a 25-table seating area with food and beverage service that became the social center of the business. The change, which enabled staff and customers to engage in new and exciting ways that benefitted everyone, was not directly about social media, but that layer of abstraction made it a more powerful story.

Presenting the idea of social in a way the audience doesn't expect can help keep the focus on the larger lesson. From there, you can delve into a specific project or technology and explore how that lesson may be applied to different scenarios.

The good news is that you can find stories everywhere. I found this one while watching TV, on a business reality show on CNBC called *The Profit*.

The story of Amazing Grapes made for a good episode, and it actually contained a number of possible lessons beyond how I presented it. The story contained lessons on business strategy, leadership, communication, customer engagement, organizational change, and even inventory management.

When you find a good story, look for the possible lessons. Or, if you have a lesson in mind, look for possible stories that can help you demonstrate the lesson.

The stories are everywhere — in the news, books, conversations, experiences, or in the plethora of links in your social media feeds. Be on the lookout and you'll soon start to notice many that can be adapted to your communications needs.

Keep an eye out and see what you find. You might be amazed.

TAKE ACTION

Find at least three good stories this week that you could use to make a point. Remember, you can look for a story to fit an idea or find a good story and shape it to an idea.

26. GIVE AN ANCHOR TO KEEP THEIR ATTENTION AFLOAT

Tell them the point, then fill in the details.

I used to always start at the beginning.

I always thought that I needed to explain things completely in order to get someone to understand an issue. So, I'd fill them in on the background, explain the fundamentals, and bring them up to speed on every step I'd taken so far.

Then, and only then, I thought, could we get into the meat and potatoes of whatever it was that needed to be discussed and decided.

Bleh.

Not effective. Not efficient.

The whole time I'm babbling, the other person is wondering what this is all about. They don't have a good way to discern important details from unimportant details at that point. They are accumulating questions, losing focus, and probably just trying to figure a graceful way out of the conversation.

I had much better luck once I figured out that the best way to start was often at the end.

If I got to the point quickly, whoever I was speaking to was much better prepared to engage.

Because I've given them an anchor.

They now had an important reference point to help them focus more directly on the most important details of the background information. They would listen more carefully and, more often than not, start asking questions.

By giving them the bottom line up front, I didn't lose my big punch line — I gained their attention.

The conversation would more naturally flow back and forth. Questions would arise that uncovered the most important background information. Details would get discussed that are most relevant to go-forward planning and strategy.

Very effective. Very efficient.

TAKE ACTION

Practice starting at the end and notice how it engages people more directly and completely. Tell one story per day that starts with the point and then fills in the details. Even incidental opportunities such as "How was your day?" or "How was your weekend?" are good places to practice.

27. GRAB IT RIGHT AWAY

G rab it! Then, they will give it to you.

I'm talking about attention.

I used to think that when it was my time to give a presentation that others would naturally give me their attention.

The idea of all eyes on me made me very nervous.

I'd worry that they would be watching my every move and hanging on my every word.

I'd worry that my clothing would be disheveled or that I'd say a lot of nervous "uh" and "um" sounds.

I'd worry whether my facts were accurate, whether my slides were numbered properly, and whether I had all sorts of relevant but trivial details memorized.

I focused on all the wrong things.

What I should have worried about was how to command the group's attention — how to grab it and how to keep it.

The attention doesn't come automatically or easily. Anything beyond polite curiosity must be earned.

Which is why strong openings are important.

If you can grab attention effectively at the beginning of your presentation, you will have a better chance of keeping it throughout the presentation.

A strong opening sets the tone — it says that you have come prepared and that you are fully engaged. It signals that you may be worth more than just polite curiosity. You might actually have something interesting to say.

Skip boring introductions and dive right in.

Open with a quote, then talk about how it applies to the theme of what you will cover.

Share a story about a customer, a partner, or yourself that resonates with some aspect of your presentation.

Raise a thought-provoking question, one that will be answered in your talk.

Open with a quote that highlights a key insight.

Use humor if the joke makes a point that's relevant (not just to "warm up the room").

Ask the audience a direct question or take a poll on an issue.

You have a lot of tools at your disposal. Select one that is appropriate for your presentation and figure out how to incorporate it in the opening of your talk.

Practice that opening, even if you don't rehearse the rest of what you'll say. Repeat it, refine it, and get comfortable with it so that you can start off on a confident and compelling note.

You likely have some sort of presentation to make soon. Even if it's just a small group discussion, a regular staff meeting, or even lunch with friends, try this technique out.

Think about what you'll talk about and then come up with a strong opening. Work up an introduction that grabs some attention. Try it out and see what sort of reaction you get.

TAKE ACTION

Create a strong opening for your next presentation. Skip introductions and warm ups and engage the audience immediately. If you need a small transition, use 30 seconds of silence where you stand quietly and simply make eye contact with the audience.

28. HOW TO MAKE A STRONG PROPOSAL

When you need to gain approval for a course of action, you'll likely need to make a presentation to a decision-maker or group of decision-makers at some point in the process.

The decision-makers will rely on the information in your presentation, and also on input and counsel from others who have a stake in the outcome.

For these reasons, the best bet is to make sure the presentation is founded on a solid argument.

To get others to pursue a course of action, they must be persuaded by a clear and compelling directive. What exactly is the argument for (or against)? How can it be boiled down to make a single point, guided by a central thesis, that fits into a specific context? How is the case for this best structured? How can it be embodied in a cohesive story? And how does it lead to a necessary action?

Answer these questions and your presentation will be pretty convincing.

Of course, that's not enough. Your presentation also needs to be defensible. After all, your audience is obligated to challenge you. They need to make sure what you're asking them to do makes sense. They need to make sure that your argument is worthy of their stamp of approval, and that it's shaped to meet their needs and interests as well as those of their constituents.

Be prepared for scrutiny.

What are the counter-arguments to your main points? What alternatives have you considered? What research supports your findings? What parts of your presentation are weak, and how will you defend them? How will your presentation remain compelling under scrutiny, now and over time (as it becomes the historical record of the decision)?

Answer these questions and be able to defend your position.

Go in with a good offense and a good defense and you'll increase your odds of a win.

TAKE ACTION

Practice making your case compelling and defensible for your next presentation. You can also revisit a past presentation and explore how you could make it stronger. Look at it from all angles. Consider all perspectives.

29. PRE-MEETING TALK STRATEGIES

If you had a chance to pull someone aside before a big meeting, what would you say to them?

Years ago, I was ramping up for a particularly important budget meeting. There was a lot on the line for my department and many choices to be made. Those choices would be made almost exclusively by the CEO, but always with input from the top leaders in the organization.

I realized that one of the ways I could influence the outcome was to influence the influencers. So I thought a lot about what I would say if I bumped into them in more informal settings.

One strategy I used for this big meeting was to send out a lot of information in advance to the people who will be there. Busy executives don't have much time to study the details, but sending the information gave me a great opening when I ran into future attendees.

Did you have a chance to look at what I sent out? No? That's OK, I can give you a brief synopsis....

This gave me the opportunity to chat up the major points I wanted to make in advance. I could express my opinions on what I thought was most important, how certain aspects of the discussion should be framed, and which items might be the best ones to defer for future budget years. I would do this all as part of my presentation, of course, but that would be in a group setting. Catching people one-on-one gave me a huge advantage.

First of all, I'd get a preview of their individual questions. Things they'd want to know but might not necessarily want to bring up in the meeting. If I didn't have the answer on the spot, I certainly would by meeting time. I could simply embed those points right in my presentation.

Second, I'd get them thinking about the issues. I would be able to influence that thinking. I would be able to make a quick pitch, hopefully provocative enough to get the wheels spinning in a certain direction.

Finally, these little vignettes gave me a chance to establish a personal connection on these topics with individual attendees. Once you've broken bread (or poured coffee or walked across the parking lot, etc.) with someone over a particular topic, the tone of your exchanges on that topic changes (usually for the better).

All of this pre-meeting talk made for a more productive and successful meeting for everyone. Each person was better informed and prepared for the meeting, and good decisions were made.

TAKE ACTION

Connect with at least three attendees in advance of a meeting this week. Find out what they are thinking. Share some of your thoughts with them. After the meeting, consider how your individual interactions informed the meeting and influenced individual roles, particularly yours and those you had pre-meeting talks with.

30. SAY IT OUT LOUD

Practice creates comfort.

When the stakes are high for a presentation, we know we should practice. And we know that practice should include an actual run-through of the talk—a dress rehearsal of sorts.

Even if just in front of the mirror or the cat, actually giving your speech helps you finalize and fine-tune it. Moreover, it helps you get comfortable.

I do this all the time for important talks and presentations. The kids have become accustomed to hearing Dad speaking to himself in the other room when a talk is coming up.

Practice does not necessarily make perfect, though it goes a long way toward feeling out the right order of things, smoothing out transitions, and selecting the right words and phrases.

Beyond fine-tuning, practice creates comfort. As I work through a talk—by actually saying it out loud, repeatedly—I get a lot more comfortable. Comfortable with the content, the structure, and the delivery.

This preparation technique works well for public speaking or high-stakes presentations. But it also works well for many smaller tasks too.

Let me walk you through a simple example.

For a new class I was about to teach at Northeastern University, I put together an introductory video. I wanted to keep it short, to briefly introduce myself and the course and to tie in the heavy online component that would be part of our study.

I wrote out the bullet points of what I wanted to cover. I then took those points and talked them through, out loud. At first, I sounded very clunky. I hesitated, wandered off topic, and stumbled.

I tried again. And again. And again. Each time, I became more comfortable with the talk, and I refined the ideas I wanted to get across and the way I wanted to deliver them. After about five attempts, I had worked my way up to a pretty good rhythm and a smooth delivery.

That may sound like a lot of effort, but practicing a three-minute introductory talk five times took only 15 minutes.

I turned on the camera and recorded a few takes before I was happy with the result. That took a little more time and effort, but the total was still less than a half hour.

More importantly, the quality improved immensely. My final recording was light-years ahead of where I started.

All it took was a little focused practice. Out loud.

Try practicing out loud for one of your upcoming talks or presentations (or even just part of it, like the introduction).

TAKE ACTION

Practice your next presentation out loud at least three times. Notice the types of changes you are able to make in order to improve your talk. Try recording on audio or video. What additional improvements were you able to make by reviewing a recording of your practice?

31. AUDIENCE FOCUS

Why aren't people giving you their full attention?

You've worked hard to prepare a thoughtful, thorough, and coherent presentation. The topic is important. Care was taken to coordinate the calendars of all the right people to be in attendance.

People are busy, but it's not their smartphones or laptops that are distracting them now.

It's your own presentation—because you gave them handouts at the start of the meeting, and that killed your momentum before it ever had a chance to build.

Focus is lost as individuals page through your work, flipping ahead to preview points, examining the bottom-line findings or costs, and exploring other details.

To keep any hope of commanding the attention of your audience, do not pass out handouts of your presentation in advance!

Bill Gates invented PowerPoint* so that you could show the presentation on screen—where you can control exactly what is revealed and when it is revealed. Don't give up that control.

If you need people to review details in order to be prepared for the meeting, by all means send out information in advance.

If you need people to study the information you're providing for further reflection, discussion, or analysis, you can send it out after your presentation. You can even hand them hard copies as they leave the room.

Keep your presentation on screen and keep control of the conversation. Keep your audience focused on each point as you present it. Be sure to present those points in a compelling way, and you'll keep their attention on you (and away from smartphones and other distractions).

Do that one thing and your next presentation will go much more smoothly.

(*I know that Bill Gates did not invent PowerPoint and that it was a product acquired by Microsoft way back in 1987.)

TAKE ACTION

Keep your slides on the screen for your next presentation. Do not give out any handouts. Notice how this changes the flow of the meeting and the attentiveness of the group.

32. HOW TO PREPARE FOR A BOARD-LEVEL PRESENTATION

It's always a struggle to figure out how to convey information effectively.

Board presentations, whether to the full board or one of its committees, present special challenges.

Material has to be high-level but also contain substance. The agenda is long and your time slot is short. Meeting cadence and decorum are long-established yet you're an infrequent participant.

What's the best way to meet this type of challenge?

Here are three ideas from my approach that may help.

1. Embrace the constraints

There's a lot about the meeting that is well beyond your control. Materials may be organized in a way that you don't like. The meeting may require a presentation style that is not your first choice. You may not be terribly familiar with the audience, individually or as a group.

That's all unfortunate, but it's also not going to change. Focus on what you can control and optimize that.

Take care to wordsmith more than usual. Spend time considering the questions that may arise. Talk to others who've presented to the group previously and get their tips and insights.

Remember: small changes can make a big difference. Seek to optimize.

2. Time yourself

These are busy people with a full agenda. You've been allotted a time slot to cover your topic. Respect that by being prepared.

High-level presentations are not the time to guesstimate. Applying a general rule of thumb based on the number of slides is not a good idea.

Besides, you need to practice anyway.

Yes, if there's only one presentation that you'll actually rehearse for this year, make it your appearance at a board meeting.

Once you have your content organized, rehearse. Rehearse until your delivery is smooth and confident. And make sure you are able to cover your material in the time you've been given.

Be practiced, be confident, be on time.

3. Convey one idea per slide

The most important thing you need to focus on is organizing your content. After all, that's what is driving your whole presentation.

Keep it clean and simple. Keep it to one idea per slide.

This will help you keep your material clear and organized. It will keep your cadence smooth and even. It will help your message stay high-level and crisp.

This doesn't mean that you can't have multiple bullet points on a slide. It means that those points should all be directly related to a single idea.

Don't transition to new ideas within a slide. Make those the transition to the next slide.

Try to keep your opening and closing slides to a single idea too. Ideally, the first slide poses the big question or idea or challenge you're about to discuss, and the final slide brings things to a resolution (or presents a single call to action of some kind).

TAKE ACTION

Deliver a talk on-point and on-budget. Keep the presentation strictly to one idea per slide. Be as professional as possible, even if it isn't a real board meeting.

33. THE BIGGEST QUESTION YOU MUST ANSWER

I know I understand something when I can explain it to someone else.

Teaching in graduate schools over the last few years has made this clearer to me than ever before.

I teach because I want to learn. I want to learn the material I already know, and process it more fully and deeply than before.

That's a nice goal for me, but what about the students?

I'd like them to know what I know. After all, that's the point isn't it? To transfer knowledge.

Actually, I've come to realize that's not the point at all.

What I have learned is that the real goal is to cause them to understand something. And to have them understand the material well enough that they can put it to effective use. Because then they will be able to learn more—much more—through their own experience.

They will be able to posit theories, test assumptions, and gain a working knowledge that leads to deeper understanding.

Isn't that how you've gained some of your deepest knowledge?

When I think about it, that's the only way I've really learned anything.

So the big lesson-design question changes dramatically. The question is no longer "What do I want them to know?" but rather "What do I want them to be able to do?"

Using that stake in the ground as a strategic objective completely changes the way I approach presenting information, designing exercises, and arranging discussions.

Now I realize that the "What do I want them to know?" question is what leads to boring and ineffective presentations, lackluster dialogue, and meatless meetings.

I've wasted hours, days, and years trying to get others to know stuff that I know — which has been the wrong goal.

The better question — and the one I ask myself much more often now — is, "What do I want them to be able to do?"

Do I want them to be able to support my initiative? Advocate for funding? Perform better in their own role? Pick option A over option B? Ask insightful questions that help set a good strategic direction?

Whatever it is, I want them to be able do something — not simply to know something.

Better goals lead to more effective communication, just like any other strategic planning exercise.

So much of learning is about asking the right questions. Turns out, it's a crucial part of teaching as well (and of course, communicating in general).

TAKE ACTION

Organize your next presentation around the question, "What do I want them to be able to do as a result of my presentation?"

34. HOW TO BECOME A BETTER PRESENTER

How have I become a better presenter?

In some ways, there's a lot to it. Like golf, there are a million things to keep in mind when preparing for and making a presentation.

And like golf, thinking about all that stuff all the time will screw up your game.

I've read books and blog posts and followed many, many tips. In the end, there was one thing that mattered most.

Just like golf...or many other things in life.

To become a better presenter, I gave more presentations.

That's the single biggest thing I've done to improve.

When I'm golfing with someone who is very good, I always ask them how often they play.

The answer is usually, "Not much...only two or three times a week."

I play two or three times a year. That's why I stink and they are very good.

It's not the only reason, but it's the BIGGEST reason.

The best thing I could do to close the skills gap between the good golfer and me would be to play more.

If I played two or three times a week for a year, I still might not be able to beat them.

But I GUARANTEE that the match would be a heck of a lot closer.

So, when I wanted to become a better presenter some years ago, I knew that the most important thing I could do was to give more presentations.

There were opportunities to do more presentations at work, and I took them. To gain more experience, however, I went further.

I needed opportunities outside of my day job that would give me a chance to present to different audiences on different topics.

And wouldn't you know it? As soon as I started looking for those opportunities, I found them.

Through my professional associations, my network, and actively pursuing speaking engagements at local conferences, I found lots of opportunities to give presentations to all sorts of audiences on all sorts of topics and in a variety of formats.

That's a bit of a scattered approach, but it worked for me because what I wanted most was raw experience. Through all of that experience, I learned lots of lessons firsthand.

As a side benefit, I gained some exposure, which led to more opportunities to make more presentations, including landing a teaching job (presenting week in and week out) and speaking gigs at industry conferences, including keynotes.

I've had a chance to try many techniques, tips, and ideas. A lot of stuff I try doesn't work, and there's some angst and aggravation along the way. It's not always that easy, but because I keep at it, I keep getting better.

TAKE ACTION

Scour your local area and find venues where you can practice your presentation skills. Look for a meetup, a conference, a networking or business group, or adult education center that is looking for volunteer speakers. Volunteer or apply to give at least three talks.

SECTION FIVE
Writing Skills

35. DOES YOUR INBOX STINK?

I try to make my messages easy to use. I think it's well worth the effort, particularly if the matter is of any importance. It helps to keep things moving along.

I certainly appreciate receiving messages that are clear and to the point. I know what they're saying (or asking) and it's easy to figure out what to do next.

If you take a scroll through your inbox, how many messages are well-written and actionable? How many stink?

If your inbox looks anything like mine, many stink. The stinky ones seem to be dashed off in haste, a jumble of thoughts that require extra effort to interpret, or some back-and-forth to clarify things.

As a writer, I try to avoid this whenever possible. I find that if I take a little extra time and effort up front, my messages can be more clear, more complete, and more compelling. It's the writer's job, in my opinion, to make things easy on the reader. It shows respect, and I think it earns respect too.

TAKE ACTION

Examine 30 messages from your current inbox. How many stink? What is it about them that makes them ineffective, unhelpful, rude, or otherwise problematic? How many are good messages? What is it about them that are helpful, informative, useful, and engender positive feelings about the author? Turn these observations into a do and don't list for the emails that you write.

36. ALWAYS RE-READ BEFORE HITTING SEND

Email is a double-edged sword.

Wonderfully and magically, we can reach out to each other instantly at any time.

Email is fast, fun, and productive. And also dangerous.

It can be too fast. Fun intent can be misconstrued.

Miscommunication at the speed of email can lead to a productivity death spiral as time and energy is diverted to clear up the confusion.

I receive a lot of email. Some do not come across so well. Often, I can figure out what the person meant. I can read the tone favorably. I can be forgiving. I try to read between the lines.

But I can also get confused, frustrated, and disappointed when the message comes across wrong.

In those cases I often think it would have been better if the sender had just picked up the phone. Or waited a little more patiently for a response. Or revised the email before sending it along.

As the recipient, I can see that plain as day. Which is why I try to avoid being the author of those messages whenever possible.

The best way I know how is to do all the things I wished others would have done before sending those bad emails to me. I try to slow down and think if a phone call might be better. Or if I should be a little more patient in waiting for a response. Or if I should review and edit the email one more time before sending it.

Email is asynchronous. Errors can't be detected and corrected immediately the way they can in a live conversation. So I find it best to try and read and review with the recipient in mind. If I were them, what would I think of this message? Is it clear? Can it be easily misconstrued?

We're all busy, but sometimes a little investment up front in clarifying the content and adjusting the tone actually saves time and energy.

TAKE ACTION

Re-read every single email you write this week before sending it. Make changes for clarity, accuracy, and tone. Notice what you learn and how much better your email writing habits are at the end of just one week.

37. THE LIMITATIONS OF EMAIL

Email is a great way to communicate information, but not a great way to communicate complex ideas or the emotional content of your message.

Unfortunately, work email has become the default mechanism to transmit anything and everything.

You likely fall into the trap of over-emailing as well. I know I do. But there are times when it pays to be more selective.

If there's more than one back and forth to clarify something, it's time to pick up the phone or meet face to face. Same goes for when messages start to get tense or emotional. When someone is confused or frustrated or outright upset, it's likely that you're not going to clear things up with more email. Some limitation of the medium likely led to the problem in the first place—or helped to make it worse.

When email replicates live conversation, it's hard enough to get the verbal translation to work well. A few strategic uses of emoticons (or parenthetical side comments) will never convey all the non-verbal cues. Think about email sent and received separately over some span of time. Then think about a phone call and how much more is conveyed by the switch to a real-time conversation and the addition of cues like tone of voice, laughter, and pauses. Then think about face-to-face conversation and how much more is conveyed there—facial expressions, body language, gestures, and more.

Email is the default link because it's fast, efficient, and convenient.

But it's also the weakest link from a communications standpoint.

Use it for what it's good at, but don't get stuck in it. Upgrade to something better when you need to tackle more complex communications challenges (which is probably more often than you think).

TAKE ACTION

Avoid email and schedule a meeting or live discussion for complex issues or anything that might be emotional or substantially nuanced.

38. THE KEY TO GOOD WRITING

How many emails do you write in a given work day?

My guess is a lot. Some studies say we spend about a quarter of our work time writing emails every day.

The pace can be frenetic at times, which is why typos, poor punctuation, and incomplete thoughts permeate many of our missives.

This is, of course, a mistake that multiplies in many cases. Every miscommunication requires more communication to explain, clarify, justify, retract, retrace, debate, or re-create. Thus the email snowball is born and set to spiral out of control (especially the ones that contain mixed metaphors!).

Better to be clear up front. Pretty much every email you write should be edited before you hit the send button.

A good rule of thumb is to correlate the number of edits to the number of recipients. A single edit for a single recipient, a few edits for a small group, and more edits for larger or more formal groups.

It's a strategic investment...measure twice and cut once.

Clarity.

Clear, complete, and accurate. That's a great place to start.

Sincerity.

That's the next step to good writing. When I write messages that don't sound like me, I've missed the mark and impeded communication.

Writing the way I speak helps immensely. Sure, formality is important in many messages, but when it goes too far, something is lost.

It's not really authentic.

This is where multiple edits can help greatly. Sometimes I'll start by writing in a very formal manner and then back it off in the edits. If I wouldn't say it out loud in a conversation, I make changes until it does sound authentic to me.

Sometimes I'll write like I speak, and the end result is too casual. In those cases, I'll re-write toward formality until I get the tone right.

It's always worth the extra effort to be clear and sincere.

TAKE ACTION

As you review drafts of your emails this week, as yourself if they are both clear and sincere. Is what you are attempting to convey crystal clear? Is the message written in your authentic voice?

39. WHAT YOU CAN LEARN FROM HEMMINGWAY

For sale, baby shoes, never worn.

This six-word novel, the legendary result of Ernest Hemingway's bet with friends, demonstrates that big stories can be delivered in small packages.

We don't have to be literary luminaries, but we can certainly benefit ourselves and our organizations by crafting similar messages to convey important ideas at work.

For crucial messages, it is important to be concise but also vivid in our descriptions.

What can we learn from Hemingway?

Immediately we grasp the sentiment of this tragic tale. That, to me, is the key — to not try and convey volumes of information but to get the point across quickly.

Metaphors are one way we can do this at work. I've described the justification for large projects in this manner. When I've conveyed that an existing system is like the Titanic just after having hit the iceberg, the sentiment is clear. We need to rescue our passengers (data) before its too late, and repairing the ship is not an option.

Once the point is made, it is easy to elaborate. And it is easy to tie everything back to that main point.

In this way, we've packaged the idea for easy consumption. We've made it memorable and easy to relay.

So here's a challenge for you:

Find something you want to describe and come up with at least three different ways to describe it.

Perhaps you want to characterize a particular challenge, justify a certain strategy, or convince others to embrace your vision of a new opportunity.

Whatever it is, aim to describe it as concisely and vividly as possible. Come up with at least three different options, ideally using different approaches.

You might try using a metaphor or analogy for one description. You might try to formulate a story for another description. You might try emphasizing a single, specific element to capture attention and convey the essential concept ("it's like 1,000 songs in your pocket").

Jot down ideas throughout your experiment (over the course of the week would work), and review them to see which might work best. You don't have to actually use them or show them to anyone (though it's always a great idea to get feedback).

Simply get some practice, and work to develop different techniques.

TAKE ACTION

Practice describing things concisely and vividly. Experiment by taking one idea and coming up with at least three different ways to describe it. Explore three completely different approaches before you decide which one will work best.

40. SMALL WORDS PACK A BIGGER PUNCH

I used to spend a lot of time with fancy words.

In fact, I still do. I like the nuance of expression that's possible with expansive and sophisticated language. Words like obfuscate, obliterate, and obviate can really dial in a sentiment. These words are really precise.

But they're not powerful. They're not persuasive.

I have spent a lot of time and energy carefully deploying sophisticated language in all sorts of communications over the years. When I've done this with written or verbal communication, I usually feel really smart. I've probably even impressed a few people.

Eventually I figured out that while I may have felt smart, I wasn't being smart.

Because what I wanted to do in these communications was influence people. I wanted them to adopt my viewpoint or support my idea, not impress them with my command of language.

Eventually I figured out that simple is more powerful than complex verbiage, because simple words are clear. Simple words speak more directly to a base emotion. And it's emotion that moves people to act.

So now I'm more likely to use "confuse" instead of "obfuscate," "destroy" instead of "obliterate," and "prevent" instead of "obviate." Less poetic but more effective in the world of work.

To get movement and momentum, a blunt instrument is often better than a precision tool. To convey big ideas, it's often better to paint a picture with broad strokes. To be clear and compelling, it's often better to speak to the underlying emotions than the rational surface layers.

Try it out this week. Take an issue where you're trying to influence the outcome and talk about it and write about it in plain and simple language. Be professional, but be blunt. Use small words that carry a big punch.

See what kind of reactions you start to get. See which of your words and phrases get picked up and repeated by others. See if you can get some momentum.

Use small words. Get a bigger reaction.

TAKE ACTION

Use simple language. Go a whole week without using any fancy words. Speak plainly. Write plainly. Keep it simple. Notice how powerful that can be.

41. TO MAKE IT NICE, WRITE IT TWICE

Write it. Then right it.

Communicating in writing is tricky. You've got to commit and then you've got to send what you've written along.

Your writing must stand on its own and represent you and your ideas well.

It's a tall order and one that I've struggled with immensely over the years. How the heck do I get the information across in a persuasive and engaging manner? How do I influence someone's thinking? What can I do to make my writing more effective?

One thing I've learned is that I can't get it right the first time. So I don't worry about that anymore.

I just write.

Then I go back and make it "right"…as in clear, compelling, and concise.

The first time around is a good opportunity to see what I'm thinking, to organize my thoughts in a concrete manner, to see them in black and white.

Then I can circle back and edit. The key is to edit ruthlessly.

I get rid of the parts where I rambled or repeated myself. I rearrange the order of sentences and paragraphs to improve the flow. I add chunks where things were thin. I drop stuff that doesn't directly support my main points.

If there's time (and it's always worth taking the time), I'll put it down for a while and come back to it later. I'll also print it out and look at it in hardcopy for a final review.

I tweak and tune until I get it just right. Once I'm happy that the writing will be easy to digest, clearly understood, and represent my ideas well, I send it along.

Writing well is really all about editing well.

Take your next writing project and get a draft out. Then, set it aside. Come back to it later and re-work it.

Switch the format to get a fresh look. If you draft on a computer, print it out to review it. If you scratch out the first draft with pen and paper, type it up to review it.

Change things around until you are convinced that what you've written will be clear and compelling. Add important elements that you missed. Even more important: take out all the junk that doesn't matter and that just distracts from your core message.

By doing this, you will represent yourself and your ideas much more effectively than if you just pass along your initial draft of a lightly edited version.

You only get one chance to make a first impression with your piece of writing. Take some extra time to put your best work out there.

TAKE ACTION

For your next writing project, create a complete first draft as quickly as possible. Don't overthink any part of it, just write it all out. Then set it aside for at least a day or two. Go back and edit it heavily in order to create a better version.

SECTION SIX

Leadership

42. HOW TO START SMART

Things can go off the rails quickly when communications aren't clear.

As things get underway, we can find ourselves caught off-guard. We can find ourselves surprised. We can find ourselves frustrated.

That's because some things turn out to be less clear than they seemed at the beginning. Things start to get a bit murky. Or maybe downright muddy.

We find that important details were not discussed at the beginning.

We figure out that some things have been misinterpreted.

We realize that we didn't point out something crucial.

We discover that we didn't ask some important questions.

I've been down this path many times. It's caused a few spills along my journeys. Those pitfalls can be painful, but they're always instructive.

If we embrace the lessons, much of the confusion can be avoided.

The biggest lesson is to simply take a little extra time at the outset. To start smart.

As we're deciding on a course of action — but before we embark on it — let's make sure as many of the essentials are as clear as possible.

Let's decide how we're going to proceed. Let's be clear on goals. Let's be clear on parameters. Let's be clear on definitions. Let's be explicit.

Sometimes this can feel like we're slowing things down unnecessarily. But that time is an investment. The payoff comes in the form of efficiency and focus and far less frustration, because we're removing ambiguity.

In fact, it makes sense to also include some check-points in our plan. We can use those as a way to ensure that everyone stays on the same page. If all is going well, the check-point provides a quick reaffirmation. If things do need to be adjusted, we have a forum where things can be clarified.

It's best to be in agreement about as much as possible up front. To make sure things are really clear even when they already seem to be pretty clear. To verify understanding. To validate parameters. To anticipate decisions and establish some guidelines.

Try it out for yourself.

Take a small project that you're going to lead and dedicate some extra time to explicitly state its goals and objectives. Verify that everyone is clear on roles and responsibilities. Make sure everyone understands the guidelines.

State things out loud that you might be tempted to leave unspoken. What seems obvious to you may not be obvious to everyone. What seems obvious to others may not be obvious to you. Ferret that out with a little discussion.

State everything as explicitly as you can. Ask questions. Invite questions.

Start smart. Finish strong.

TAKE ACTION

Be clear up-front about the very next thing you start this week. Make sure that everyone has a clear understanding of the goal, the approach, and the reasons why the project is being undertaken. Take extra time to verify that these details are unmistakably clear.

43. WHY YOU SHOULDN'T TRY TO GET IT RIGHT THE FIRST TIME

Start early, revise often.

Too many times, I've waited until the last minute to complete something.

Cramming does work.

Compressing all of my effort and energy into the work so that it can be completed just-in-time is an effective style.

It forces focus. Focus fuels concentration and deep thinking.

The results can be good.

That's how I got through most of college, and it's how I've done many things in my work life.

Until I learned the power of iteration.

And how iterating can make results much, much better.

Now, whenever I've got something important to work on (which is most of the time — why work on something unimportant?), I start early.

It's always rough in the beginning. The first try is often light years from where things need to land. But there is power in simply starting. A lot of power.

As writer Anne Lamott so eloquently puts it, we need to create shitty first drafts. Quality isn't important on the first run-through. It's important to get started and compose a complete set of thoughts.

Once we do that, we can simply set it aside. That's why it's important to start early. We need to let our subconscious chew on the thing for a bit. And, rest assured, it will.

Ideas, insights, concepts will emerge when you least expect them, usually while you're occupied with something else. That's why we get so many good ideas in the shower, while mowing the lawn, or during our morning run.

The important thing is to provide some fuel. That fuel is a first draft, a sketch, a model, a prototype.

Don't put off thinking something through. Don't make a big deal out of it. Don't plan to cram.

Plan to let it stew. Cut up some raw materials, throw them together, and let them simmer for a while. Allow yourself to come back and make adjustments over time, even radical ones like completely re-arranging things or starting over from scratch.

You might throw out some stuff along the way, change your mind about certain aspects, or decide to completely re-approach the matter. All of that will make the final product better.

But you'll never get there if you don't allow for it. If you plan to cram, you've likely eliminated lots of possibilities, and chances are some of those possibilities would be great.

So, try this week-long exercise. Let's say you have something that needs to be done by Friday. Create a rough draft or outline your thoughts on Monday. It's important to take concrete action — don't just think about it, actually write this stuff down.

Then, set it aside. Think about it intentionally here and there, but also let yourself forget about it and see what pops into your mind over time.

Revisit it on Wednesday. Revise it on Thursday, and a couple times more on Friday.

See how it looks.

Did it come out better than if you had waited until the last minute and crammed?

TAKE ACTION

Take something you have to complete in the coming weeks and start on it right now. Begin a process of iteration and improve your work incrementally. Make drastic changes if necessary, but continue to build on your past work.

44. CLEAR UP COMMUNICATIONS GAPS WITH A VIRTUAL CAMPFIRE

It's good to gather people around the virtual campfire.

Whatever the project or team, there's always a need to gather face-to-face. Outlook and Basecamp and texting help us to communicate. Microsoft Project and Excel, Google Docs, and Evernote help us to keep track of things and to collaborate.

Today's tools are a boon and I wouldn't want to try to do without them. It's important to remember, though, that they have their limits. They leave gaps, they are misused, and they can never fully replicate in-person exchanges.

There's nothing quite like gathering together and speaking live.

Of course, we do this all the time in formal meetings. Those serve a valuable purpose too. But they have their limitations as well. Structure and protocol can hinder some important elements of communication.

Less formal gatherings and discussions help fill the gaps.

We humans are natural communicators. We're used to gathering around the campfire and discussing the events of the day and our plans for the future.

Gathering in a similar way around a particular topic or project can really help communication flow more effectively. The key, I've found, is to keep the feel of the campfire: a communal experience where hierarchy is ignored and everyone can contribute to the conversation.

When this sort of conversation gets flowing, it's amazing what you can learn from your fellow campers. It's amazing what you can convey, quickly and easily. It's amazing how many little gaps can be filled in. Which helps all the tools and formal meetings become that much more effective.

TAKE ACTION

Call your group together for an informal meeting. Order in pizza. Go out for beer. Share dessert. Create an excuse to gather and speak freely about whatever challenges you are facing.

45. TRY TO SIT QUIETLY FOR 5 MINUTES

Five minutes is actually a long time.

It's enough time to make a fresh fruit smoothie in your blender, fill your gas tank, and grab a gallon of milk at the station, read a 1,500-word article, or listen to Rihanna's song "Umbrella" from beginning to end — with 24 seconds to spare!

Using five minutes strategically, to prepare for an upcoming meeting, can be a huge boost to effectiveness in the meeting.

Of course, I spend a lot more time preparing for meetings that I'm leading. What I'm talking about here is meetings that I'm attending as a participant.

I like to be a smart and helpful contributor.

To do that, I used to set the bar very high, and often I'd miss the mark. I'd want to spend a lot of time preparing in detail, but I'd end up doing no preparation.

Then I discovered the power of preparing better by simply thinking deliberately about the meeting for just a short amount of time. Even five minutes of focused reflection before the meeting makes a big difference.

Resisting the urge to check email or squeeze in last minute tasks between meetings, I'll often spend a few minutes in quiet reflection.

I noticed that when I do that for even just five or 10 minutes, I perform much better in that meeting.

I communicate my ideas more clearly. I've given them a little thought and I'm not speaking entirely off the cuff.

I listen to others more completely. I'm not trying to remember what happened at the last meeting or otherwise mentally catch up while someone else is talking.

I've already gathered my thoughts.

I've taken some time to think about who is attending, what I know about each person and their interests in the topic, what questions I want answered and what else I want to get out of the meeting.

I've found this particularly helpful when dealing with big concepts and complex systems. Even a short amount of mental preparation helps to get me focused on essential matters at hand and steer clear of erroneous details.

More preparation is better, and certainly called for when the stakes are high. But resisting the urge to view preparation as "all or nothing" for many meetings can make a big difference.

You can do a lot of thinking (a surprising amount) in five minutes when those minutes are focused on just one thing.

TAKE ACTION

Prior to each and every meeting this week, take five minutes to sit quietly and reflect on the topic that will be discussed. Think about the issues, your thoughts and concerns, and potential ways to move things forward.

46. THERE ARE ALWAYS ALTERNATIVES

Break away from narrow framing.

Sometimes discussions can become very narrow. Anxious to arrive at a decision and get moving with an initiative, a group can be tempted to reduce a point to its most basic form. Someone will present the issue simply as a black or white, an all or nothing, or a "do or do not" decision.

Sometimes this is helpful. Sometimes it's a trap.

Narrowly framing a decision can make the world of opportunities very small. I always like to have at least three options, and in most circumstances, it doesn't take much effort to come up with many more.

Group discussions are tricky, though. And when someone boils the matter down to a single point, it's tempting to consider that to be a level of clarity that compels action: Either we should do this thing or we shouldn't...what do you think? Individuals weigh in and a decision is made.

Sometimes it makes sense to resist this reduction. Sometimes the group hasn't looked at the issue broadly enough. Sometimes there are more options that should be considered. When that happens, I find it helpful to try and break the narrow framing.

This action is a bit risky. When I do this, I feel that I could be seen as a blocker. Someone trying to muck up the works rather than moving things forward. Someone who is complicating a simple matter.

I'll take that risk if the issue warrants it.

One of the most effective ways of speaking up in this way, I've found, is to revisit some of the parameters that are guiding the decision. Those assumptions have a huge impact. Revisiting them can shake the footing of the discussion and break the narrow frame.

What if the deadline wasn't the deadline? Or the customer behavior wasn't what we always assumed it was? Or some capability of the technology doesn't work? Or what if we consider that some aspect of corporate folklore that's always presumed but never questioned isn't what we think it is?

Many times this shakeup will lead to new ideas and inputs and concerns pretty quickly. Sometimes the assumptions are reconsidered and hold up just fine. That's OK too. The exercise has value even if it simply clarifies communications and ensures that everyone is truly on the same page.

TAKE ACTION

The next time you are in a group that is contemplating a decision, challenge one or more of the assumptions. See if a wider framing of the question can be explored. Find a way to get the group to step back and take a broader perspective.

47. WHY YOU SHOULDN'T BE SO CERTAIN ALL THE TIME

Widen the frame, check the assumptions.

I like to be certain, of course. It's great when a piece of knowledge, a concrete experience, or a indisputable fact guides my way.

That's confidence building and fun.

But it isn't always the best way to get the best results.

Many times, I'm better off being less certain, hesitating a bit, and questioning things at least a little further.

Creative and elegant and robust solutions are more apt to come from a more complete and nuanced understanding of a problem or a situation.

I'm not talking about analysis paralysis all day long...that's no good.

I'm talking about those times when something is important enough, or when something is tapping into emotions a bit more deeply than it seems it should, or when maybe the answer feels a little too obvious....

That's when it's often a good time to pause and reflect a little more deeply and ponder a few questions.

"What is the problem we are trying to solve?" Revisiting that question is a good place to start.

Further questioning helps: "Why does the problem exist?"

What is it that sets the conditions of the problem? Why are those things the way they are? Are they likely to remain intact over time?

Widening the frame to take a broader view can help uncover a perspective that more narrow framing would crop out.

Questioning the assumptions, especially the ones that aren't explicitly stated, helps to consider where things really stand right now and how they might play out over time.

Are the things we know to be true really true? Will they always be true? Why or why not? What might cause them to change?

The standard way of doing things might be fine. A commonplace view of the problem might be accurate. Characterizing things quickly might be efficient.

Introducing some uncertainty, however, might reveal more and better opportunities.

Sometimes it is a good idea to more closely examine what appear to be the foundational elements — to give 'em a little shake and see how they hold up (or don't).

A good way to play around with this idea would be to test the waters in a real life situation and ask just one more question before deciding on a course of action.

Take one of these opportunities to go one step further than you would normally.

Ask yourself one more question before you make a decision.

Ask one more question before the meeting ends.

Pretend you are your boss or your boss' boss, and ask one more question from their perspective.

Or pretend you're the customer and ask one more question.

Ask one more question that seems so obvious that it shouldn't be asked and see what happens.

Ask if anyone else would like to ask one more question.

TAKE ACTION

When you are part of a group that is tasked with coming to a decision, make sure that everyone has a clear and detailed understanding of the problem first. Spend extra time and energy asking a few more questions about the problem and the assumptions before trying to come to a conclusion.

48. SMALL CHANGES, BIG RESULTS

Innovation doesn't always need to require huge change to be impactful.

Sure, smart people are working hard to launch expeditions to Mars, transition to electric and/or self-driving cars, and to disintermediate everything (Zipcar, Uber, Airbnb, etc.). World-changing stuff.

That takes smarts and resources and willpower and drive and commitment and influence and the ability to see things that aren't there.

There's also tremendous power in simply seeing things as they are — in understanding how things work, why they are set up or operate a certain way, and how people behave in and around those things.

Shortcuts and hacks (the good kind) are the result of clever thinking based on these observations.

One clever move can produce a big leap.

If you know your environment and you know your objective, you can look for small but highly leverageable insights. Then, you can use these to advance things faster and more efficiently.

A simple example is trying to get your work done in a busy office environment.

You know you need to work on the report, but you also know that you're likely to be interrupted by phone calls, emails, and people dropping by. The breaks in concentration caused by all those interruptions are a problem.

You can get mad and frustrated because it's impossible to change the environment or the need to get the report done.

Or you can change the rules of the game. At least for you and at least for a little while.

Isolating yourself for an hour by shutting your office door or commandeering a conference room, turning off phone and email (including blinky lights and popup notifications) will change the game.

This small but clever workaround will go a long way toward meeting an important goal. Being disconnected for an hour may seem weird in this day and age, but it's also weirdly empowering. If you're out of the habit of working this way, you'll be amazed at what you can accomplish in an hour of focused time.

The same idea can be scaled up to bigger objectives and larger environments. Look for the hack. Look for the shortcut. Look for the way to "beat the system" without necessarily changing the rules but by working within them, around them, or by leveraging them in new or unexpected ways for greater gain.

You won't always find a shortcut, at least not right away. Building a habit of constantly looking is still a good thing to do. The more you look, the more you will see over time.

TAKE ACTION

Hack your work environment this week. Spend one hour per day completely isolated from interruptions. Shut your office door, book a conference room, hide in a local coffee shop with headphones on. See how this impacts your productivity, creativity, and sense of control.

49. HOW TO TURN AMBIGUITY INTO ACTION

Ideas are great, but really don't stand for much on their own. They are actually quite useless if they don't get acted upon.

As the saying goes, execution eats strategy for lunch.

The challenge is that the path to execution can require moving through some ambiguity.

Often, and particularly when we're breaking new ground, it is unclear how to make the leap from ideation to action. How to take the first steps on a new and exciting journey.

Many times, this is where ideas die. Or worse, they languish indefinitely.

People can feel like the problem is solved once the idea is crystalized and then go back to the many other issues that require attention. We walk away feeling confident that it will be acted upon. After all, the idea is good and it serves an important purpose.

But who is going to initiate that action? And how are they going to do it?

Sometimes there isn't a precedent for this particular initiative or there isn't an obvious forum to bring it to or it's unclear who should "own" the next steps.

Here's where one of the best, most important, and most powerful tenets of leadership comes into play:

Make stuff up.

Yes, you're job is to invent the future, and here's the perfect opportunity to make something happen.

There is no plan? There is no precedent? There is no clear path?

Make one.

As long as you base your actions on rational thinking and develop a plan of action aimed at servicing the strategic objectives of the organization and whatever particular initiative is in play, things will be fine.

Even if your plan is imperfect.

The idea here isn't to develop a perfect end-to-end plan. What's needed is action. Action will lead to reaction, discussion, revised plans, further analysis and planning, and more action.

After all, if the idea is sound and aimed at strategic goals, the most important next step is to figure out how to make it happen. That's the conversation you're trying to incite.

The key to breaking through the ambiguity is to take the first step. Lots can fall into place after that. But nothing can happen without it.

So, what can you do this week to put this idea into practice?

Start small...maybe with something as simple as lunch.

The next time you're making lunch plans with a group, deviate from the ambiguity that all too often surrounds these sorts of conversations.

You know the drill. We approach the discussion tentatively and head down a path of raising more questions that don't really matter so much in the long run. "Where do you want to go to lunch?" And after all the back and forth finally settles down: "What time should we go?" Which only leads to more back and forth....

Instead of wasting time, suggest a very specific plan of action. "Let's go to Temptations Cafe at 12:30 and plan to be back at the office by 1:30."

Now, even if the location and time change in the resulting discourse, see if the group gets to action faster. Is there less back and forth? Did you help shape the path forward simply by putting a stake in the ground? By giving a specific plan for people to react to?

The objective is to enjoy a group lunch. The plan of how we get there is secondary. So, rather than put lots of energy into plan building with the group, start with a very specific draft. Even if it changes (and it will), you've helped to meet the larger goal more effectively.

And if you can do that for lunch plans, you can do that in service of other objectives as well. Start small and experiment.

TAKE ACTION

Make up a plan this week. Take the initiative to put something forward, even if you are not the official leader of the team or effort. Help everyone by putting forth a potential course of action.

50. ARE YOU ACTING OR REACTING?

A re you acting with intent, or are you just acting (which really means that you're reacting)?

I react a lot. Sometimes I overreact ;-)

In fact, it's fun to react. I love those days when you don't know what's going to happen next.

I love when there's a lot of activity and the challenge is to figure out how to dodge, duck, and dive around the obstacles. It's fun to figure out what immediate action is necessary to resolve an issue or tackle a problem that you didn't even know existed a little while ago.

There's a sense of satisfaction that comes with reacting well to immediate challenges, particularly when I can attach them to some larger goal. That justifies my actions even more.

But the truth is, it's also satisfying even if I can't tie my actions to some lofty goal.

It's satisfying because I can take action and see results right away. The immediate feedback is rewarding. That's how gamification works, and it's what gets me hooked on reacting to things even though I'm not a gamer (not since the days of the arcade version of Donkey Kong anyway).

If I do this too much, though, I find that I'm not feeling any rewards at all over the long term. I'm not feeling a sense of accomplishment from simply being busy.

Which is why I've found it to be incredibly important to be intentional.

Acting with intent is crucial for things that matter in the long term. And a lot matters in the long term.

Acting with intent is a game changer.

The amazing thing is that the shift can be subtle but still yield huge results.

It's all about mindset. It's all about shifting perspective to one that is forward-looking and focused on some larger goal. It's all about thinking about how what I'm going to do next will build to something more substantial over time. It's about pursuing a thread of thought persistently over time and throughout various endeavors.

If you go into your day with intent, there will still be all sorts of things to react to and you'll need to adjust accordingly. But you can come out the other side with at least incremental progress in a variety of areas.

First, you can control more by being intentional. A simple example is in how you start your day. If you intend to get something important done, do it first. Forgo checking your phone, watching the morning news, or stopping by the local coffee shop until you make some progress on your top priority of the day. Then, even if the rest of your day goes haywire, you've at least made progress in an important area.

Second, go into tasks with more intent. As you engage in that next meeting, do you have a longer-term goal in mind? Perhaps you want to improve a particular relationship, learn more about some specific subject area, or get feedback on a new idea. Take the opportunity to shift how you approach the meeting to work toward that longer-term goal.

Third, reflect on the day and plan for the next. As you look back on your day, use it to inform your strategies for making the most of the coming day. What intention do you want to set for tomorrow? What will be your important morning task? How will you approach some already planned activity and use it to serve longer-term goals? How will you want tomorrow to feel when you reflect back on it at the end of the day?

Try one or more of these ways to be intentional and see how it feels. See how you react.

TAKE ACTION

Start each day this week by working on your most important task first. Set everything else aside and focus at least one hour on that task.

51. WHAT IS YOUR LINE OF QUESTIONING?

I find it helpful to give some thought to driving conversations through a line of questioning aimed at specific goals. A good example is vendor presentations, particularly those where a new potential partner is learning about your organization and you're learning about theirs.

Those meetings often try to cover lots of ground in a short amount of time. Which is precisely why it's helpful to have some sort of strategy to make sure the time together is as effective as possible.

When I'm on the receiving end of a presentation, one of the best tools at my disposal is questions. With good questions, I can avoid many drab and unproductive components of a canned presentation and help make the discussion more productive for both parties.

For this to work, the questions need to be good. Which is why I take time to think through my meeting goals in advance. What do I really want to learn about this partner and how they view this opportunity? What do I really want to be sure they know about my organization? What are the key things I need to learn from this exchange? Once I've decided on (and prioritized) a set of goals, I use that framework to guide my line of questioning during the meeting.

As the meeting unfolds, I find opportunities to engage directly and meaningfully at several points through pointed questions that are all working toward the specific goals I've thought of ahead of time.

This works particularly well when vendors are knowledgeable, experienced, and well-prepared. The discussion is more dynamic but also more focused on the points that matter most. Weaker vendors tend to get exposed more readily through this approach too, which is also productive for me.

Strategy doesn't prohibit spontaneity. Lots of unexpected things can come up, and that's fine. But having this sort of meeting without a strategy can waste a lot of time.

How do you get the most out of these sorts of meetings?

TAKE ACTION

Forget about what you are going to say in meetings this week. Try to be the person who asks the best questions.

52. BODY LANGUAGE BASICS

My business coach first introduced me to the importance of body language. He was teaching me about the important nuances of sales for the consulting business I ran many years ago.

The process engaged high-level executives, often the business owners, directly in face-to-face meetings. One crucial element of those meetings that we focused on a lot was body language.

Joe explained to me that communication is more than words. What we say matters a lot, but how we say it as just as important. A big part of how we say it is through our body language.

It's also a big part of how we need to listen—by reading the signals in the body language of others.

Our body language helps to show our level of respect and authenticity. Reading their body language helps us react and adjust to unspoken feedback and concerns. All of this lays the groundwork for establishing the trust and credibility needed not just for a successful sale but for a successful, ongoing relationship.

Joe's advice has served me well. Picking up on the body language cues of others and projecting myself in specific ways through specific body language techniques has helped me tremendously over the years.

But here's the thing that's really interesting. Body language can not only help us in communicating with others, it can also help us communicate with ourselves.

The way we carry ourselves sends important signals to our bodies. For instance, we know that confident people carry themselves with open and expansive body language. Science has shown us that the opposite is also true—carrying ourselves with open and expansive body language can help us to become more confident.

If you stand for two minutes like a gymnast at the end of a routine, with your legs spread apart and arms up and open wide above your head, your testosterone level will rise and your cortisol level will fall—the same physiological response to being more confident and less nervous.

I've used this exact technique to prepare for important presentations or meetings. It's a great way to get primed for the event. Certainly much better than our default behavior of hunching over a smartphone in a very closed and confined posture.

Try it out for yourself. At your next meeting, notice who is adopting an open posture, leaning back with arms apart and shoulders squared, and who is more closed, with arms crossed and head tilted down. What are they telling you with those cues?

Notice the positions you are adopting. Notice when you are more open or closed. Experiment with a more open pose when you are speaking or listening and trying to engender trust. Put yourself in a closed position and see how others react.

And before your next big presentation or meeting, ditch the smartphone and take two minutes to purposely adopt a large and open pose to prime yourself for a confident performance.

TAKE ACTION

Observe your own body language throughout each day for an entire week. Pay careful attention to the nonverbal communication of everyone around you for the entire week. What lessons can you take from these observations?

Go Be Great!

Now is a great time to open up a whole new world of possibilities for yourself.

Wouldn't it be nice to have more possibilities?

Well, you can. Because science has actually proven that you can create your own luck. I've experienced it firsthand. It works.

That's what we've been talking about throughout this entire book.

Opportunities appear for those who are ready for them. Those who can see them. Those who can seize them.

The secret to finding new opportunities is believing that you will. The best way to do that is to develop a habit of trying new things. Put the 52 ideas in this book (at least some of them) into action.

The more you see, the more you will believe that you will see. So, the more you will see.

I will explain how it works.

Do things that help you to grow. Things that put you into new situations. Things that cause you to meet and interact with new people. Things that expose you to lots of new kinds of possibilities.

Doing this as a habit could make this your best year yet. If not the best, maybe one of the top five. But probably the best.

When you try new things, you adopt a beginner mindset. That is a mindset full of possibilities.

As you try new things, you gain new perspectives. Some of those views are completely new, and invigorating. Some reinforce similar patterns in areas where you are more experienced. Some help you to re-look at those same old areas in completely new ways, to see them with fresh eyes.

This is how you unlock insights that would otherwise elude you.

Here's an even bigger thing, though. While a new experience can be eye-opening, making a habit of creating new experiences for yourself can have a huge multiplier effect.

By doing new stuff all the time, you keep closer to the beginner mindset more of the time. You become used to trying new things. Each one becomes a little less scary or intimidating. And each time, you are rewarded with new ideas, new insights. Which helps you grow and become a little more daring. So you try more new things and keep the cycle going.

People who have experimented with this have had great results. Fantastic results. Those are the people who encourage us all to "DO EPIC SHIT!"

They are right. The key *is* to do epic shit.

My personal take on this is that you should do whatever epic means for **you**. And that you should do it repeatedly.

Epic might certainly be something outlandish like taking your first skydive. Or it might be making your first foray into public speaking.

Epic is relative. As long as it's epic for you, it counts. Massively.

Here's a good one. Try the profoundly important and often-avoided act of giving honest and direct feedback to someone who desperately needs it. That's hard. Really hard.

It's epic.

Especially if that sort of thing is new territory for you. It is for many of us. It still seems like new territory for me, no matter how often I do it. But every time I do it — every time — it's been the right thing to do. Regardless of the outcome.

That's the other thing I want to convey to you. Opening up your possibilities means just that. It's about *possibilities*, not outcomes. It's about *experiences*, not results. It's about *learning*, not knowing what's going to happen in advance.

My hope is for you to do bigger work over the next year. More important work. Your best work.

To do that, you've got to live a bigger life all-around.

Living a bigger life is all about expanding your personal horizons. Making more things possible for you and those around you. This inevitably feeds your work. It fuels your energy. It increases your capabilities.

It's about expanding your comfort zone. Because many of the limitations we face are self-imposed. We humans are very good at talking ourselves out of things.

You might be thinking about some limitations you've put on yourself right now. Some things that you wanted to try, but didn't. Something that you wanted to quit, but you continued on doing it anyway. Something that you wish was different but isn't, because you didn't even try (or you didn't *really* try).

We talk ourselves out of change all the time. Humans are great at rationalizing the status quo.

To move beyond that, we need to break the cycle.

The steps can be small. Baby steps, even. The important thing is to keep going just a little further into new territory. Habitually.

Do that little by little all year long and I guarantee you will have a great year. Maybe your best year ever.

You will grow as a person and as a professional. You will help many others around you. You will have the strength and skills to serve them better. You will be an excellent example to them.

I have some more ideas to help get you started. I've tried most of these myself. No matter how things worked out, each thing I tried helped me grow because I was trying something new. I gained new experiences. I learned new things. I met new people.

All of that has made my life bigger and my work better.

Give these ideas a go (only if you haven't done them before!):

- Join a book club where you don't know anyone

- Take a workshop to learn a new skill

- Go to a conference for a profession that is totally different than what you do in your day job (and go alone)

- Teach a class

- Take up golf

- Stop playing golf for a year (what would you do with that time?)

- Volunteer for a day

- Serve on a board or committee for an organization you are already involved in

- Read a book in a new genre

- Ditch your phone for a day

- Learn to cook

- Learn to sing

- Learn to play an instrument

- Do a set of standup comedy

- Sign up for a marathon

- Rewrite your resume (only if you're NOT looking for a new job)

- Start journaling

- Begin a new morning routine

- Go a full week without watching TV at night

- Eat lunch with someone you don't know well (yet)

- Take an online course

- Send an email to someone whose work you admire

- Write a book

- Run a 5K

- Start a blog

- Create a YouTube video

How did that list look to you? Were some things exciting? Some things scary?

Add to it. You probably already have some other ideas on what you would like to try. Things you have considered, maybe a long time ago, but just haven't tried yet.

Let your emotions guide you on what to try next. The most exciting or scary idea is probably a good place to start. Even just with baby steps.

Don't talk yourself out of it. Make a note right now of that thing you just thought of. Try it out as soon as you possibly can. Today, even.

Once you complete it, move on to another thing. Until trying new things becomes a habit.

Do this and implement your favorite ideas presented in this book. Start anywhere, but start now.

Go be great.

BONUS PDF!

Use the web address below to get a free PDF with all 52 Take Action! steps summarized neatly into one document for easy review…and action!

http://www.tomcatalini.com/CLYBonus

ACKNOWLEDGEMENTS

It's never a good idea to go it alone. People can help you make your work better. Much better. They push you. They encourage you. They make the whole process enjoyable and rewarding.

I am immensely grateful for the help I received on this project. It's humbling. And it's awesome.

Thank you.

Thank you to Sue Bergamo, Eric Bloom, Martin Davis, Omar Halabieh, Katherine MacRostie, Christopher Morgan, and David Walsh. Thanks also to Sarah Johnson and Boris Decovski for polishing things off with your deft editing and graphic design skills.

Of course, I wouldn't get anywhere without Stephanie. Or the motivation and inspiration that Alec, Mia, and Annalise provide every day.

Made in the USA
Columbia, SC
25 April 2017